ten pearls *of* wisdom

Ten Pearls
of
Wisdom

Achieving Your Goals &
Capturing Your Dreams

Eleanor Jacobs, M.S.W., L.C.S.W.

Kodansha International

New York • Tokyo • London

Kodansha America, Inc.
114 Fifth Avenue, New York, New York 10011, U.S.A.

Kodansha International Ltd.
17-14 Otowa 1-chome, Bunkyo-ku, Tokyo 112-8652, Japan

Published in 1998 by Kodansha America, Inc.
Copyright © 1998 by Eleanor Jacobs

Library of Congress Cataloging-In-Publication Data
Jacobs, Eleanor, 1943–
Ten pearls of wisdom: achieving your goals & capturing
your dreams / Eleanor Jacobs.

p. cm.
ISBN 1-56836-255-2
1. Success. I. Title.
BJ1611.J26 1998   98-18874
158—dc21   CIP

Book packaged by Livre Noir • Los Angeles, California
Design by Moira & Company • Chicago, Illinois
Manufactured in the United States of America

98 99 00 01 02   QFF   10 9 8 7 6 5 4 3 2 1

Dedicated with love and gratitude to
Robert (Bob) Jacobs, my husband,
Robert Louis Davis II, my son —
and the memory of my grandmother,
Mrs. Eleanor Brooks Johnson
(1893–1970)
and my father, Felix Charles Johnson, Jr.
(1919–1988)

Contents

$\mathcal{M}$y heartfelt gratitude goes to my dynamic literary agent, Charlotte Gusay, who believed in this book and hung in with it when the going got really, really tough; to Deborah Baker, my editor, for her enthusiasm and excellent guidance; and, also, to Philip Turner at Kodansha.

I am truly blessed to have a family of consummate cheerleaders—my husband and my son; my sister Vivian Harp, with her marvelous sense of humor; and my niece Valerie Lee. Their chorus is always joined by my California brood—Susan, John, Kate, and Chris "Little Jake" Stapp; Mindy, Bear, Samantha, Marcy, Messiah, and Charles; and Robert and Pat Davis. And then there are my Missouri cousins—Maria and Houston

Randall; Madeline and Jerome Morgan; Richcella; Francine; in memory—my cousin Rick; and our Oregon contingent—Jan and Derek Clanton, Michelle, and Nicole.

I want to say a special thank you to Adele Horwitz, my patient and world-class teacher; my mentor, Ira Okun; my "man for all seasons," Gary Marshall; Dennis Wootten, who was always there for me; and Marguerite Jensen Owens, who nourishes my spirit with her wisdom.

I have to acknowledge my gaggle of girlfriends—Carmen Fabry, Betty Waters, Mary Helen Johnson, Monica Perkins, Shirley Drake, Rosemarie Fernandez, Mabel Jung, Theo Steele, Ann Kennedy, Denise and Mama Lillie Hereford, Bea Stephens, Anne O'Shea, Mary Helen Rogers, Ilene Sapp, Karen Shea, Judy Maatz, and Barbara Thompson. If I don't, I will be drummed out of the corps.

Last but not least, kudos to Jim McCluskey and Angie Vincenti who jettisoned me out of the stone age into the wonders of technology; and Joel Campos, Alba Hernandez, and Norman Seguin, who keep me up on all the skinny.

IN A SHELL:
WHERE THIS STRAND CAME FROM,
WHAT IT IS, AND WHAT IT DOES

*I*t is 1971. Looking up from my typewriter, I glance around the busy office where I work. For the tenth or fifteenth time that day I feel a surge of discontent well up in me. Trying to shake it off, I put my fingers to my temples and hang my head for a few minutes. Finally I am able to get back to the typing.

Driving home in the rusty '55 Chevy I had bought two years before, I imagine I can smell the whiffs of carbon monoxide I had been told were seeping inside whenever I drove the car.

"Bad problem," the mechanic had said, "and it needs to be fixed fast. It'll be about four hundred dollars."

"Will it hurt me if I keep driving?"

"Sure will."

Still I hadn't done anything about it. After paying my rent, gas, and light bill out of my once-monthly paycheck of two hundred and seventy dollars, I didn't have the money.

Savings? That was a laugh. And how many times can a grown woman keep asking her father for help? I had gone to my father so many times of late that my pride had finally kicked in. Wasn't I a grown up? When was I going to be able to stand on my own?

I got home, sat on the couch in my living room, and burst into tears. Hours later I found myself still sitting there with my coat on. Finally I crawled into bed and stared at the ceiling.

"What's wrong?" I asked myself.

Only a few weeks earlier, on my twenty-eighth birthday, I had looked into the mirror and decided that I didn't look bad at all. I had a good, steady job as a clerk at the health center. My friends considered this a major achievement. Most of them were still on the jobs they had taken just out of high school.

Some of them were married and had children and still did quite well; they paid the rent on time, wore attractive clothes, and drove new cars.

I had been married. I had no children and my married friends thought that I was lucky to be able to spend my salary on just myself. What was my problem?

As far as relationships went, I was between boyfriends by choice. A month before I had ejected from my life a fellow I had been seeing who had quit the job he had when we met and was not aggressively pursuing reemployment. When he turned down a job at a neighborhood gas station because, as he put it, "I'm too good to be a gas jockey," I realized he didn't share my work ethic and that ended the relationship for me. There have been other times when I had no steady companion, so I didn't think that being single was the reason for my malaise.

"What is it then?" I asked myself as I began to doze off.

Later that night I awoke, sat up, and started to think.

"I want my life to be different, I want to be more than I am," I thought.

"But you are okay now. For someone of your class and circumstances, you're doing fine," I told myself. "You have a high school diploma and have completed a year of college. That's great. You're the only one in your crowd who has been to college at all."

Back and forth I argued, but it didn't help.

"Stop reaching," I told myself. "What you have is a lot better than what a lot of people have. Plus you've got a family and friends who like and respect you."

I got up and went to the bookshelf to find something to read.

Years later

It is 1983. I look up from my desk and survey my large, lovely office. A feeling of pride and accomplishment pervades my being and I smile.

"Well, well, well," I think, "this is success."

And it is. In the short space of twelve years, I have climbed to the top of my chosen profession. I am the executive director of an agency in one of the major social services systems in California. I am in charge of a large staff and responsible for a budget of a million dollars. My colleagues in the field concede that this kind of rise is unusual. Usually it takes two decades or more to reach the top position in my field of work.

How did it happen?

How had I done this? I was an average person from an average station in life, and I did not begin working in my profession until I was over thirty years old. Many of my fellow executives had gone to college right out of high school and to graduate school immediately after that. Plus, it usually took ten years before one even became a candidate for middle management, let alone hold the post of executive director. How had it all happened to me—and in twelve years?

Back to the bookshelf

Remember the night in 1971 when I went to the bookshelf to find something to read? Well, what I found was a book I had picked up at a garage sale about psychic power and how it can be used in everyday life to achieve everyday goals. That book equated psychic power with the gut feelings, notions, hunches, flashes, and impulses that people get that seem to come from nowhere. It explained that these instincts or intuitions are natural to all of us and that picking up on them, paying attention to what they are saying, and letting them guide us can help us as we make our way through life.

The information in that book was exciting. At an early age I knew that I got what I called impressions, a sense about the people around me or the situations I was in, from out of the blue. It felt kind of funny to me when it happened, and I usually ended up putting those thoughts aside and forgetting about them. The failure of my marriage, too, made me question myself.

After that book I started reading other self-help books. Many of them had common themes or guidelines, and I began to study certain points more frequently than others. Eventually I put those books aside and concentrated on the inspiration I received from my own heart.

My belief in myself became unshakable. That belief became the core grain of sand that I used to cultivate my pearls of wisdom.

It took time

The growing of my pearls of wisdom did not happen quickly. It was at least a year after reading that first book before I came to trust my instincts and use them on a daily basis. My self-training began like a game. I would stop myself in the middle of an activity and pay attention to what my feelings were at that moment. At first the impressions arrived sporadically. I'd stop and think, "Am I getting a hunch?" and sometimes I couldn't feel anything at all. But gradually I began to get strong, clear impressions about the situation I was in or the person I was talking to.

I'd find myself thinking about a specific course of action and the thought would occur, "No, don't do that" or "Do it this way." I'd follow through on that thought and whatever it was would turn out just the way I wanted. At work I could be finishing a report and be about to turn it in when I'd get a flash to "check page seven again." When I did, I found a mistake there, even though I thought I had proofread the document carefully.

One time I was dressing to go to a concert that I had been looking forward to and for which I had bought a very expensive ticket. As I picked up my purse and my keys I had a flash that said, "Don't go, stay home." At first I brushed it aside and told myself, "I'm going to this concert and that's that." But as I went out the door and turned to lock it, the flash came back. I stood for a few minutes, mulling it over. Then I decided to heed my hunch. I went inside, undressed, and stayed home. The next day the morning paper reported that there had been a melee at the concert and five people had been hurt. Later, talking with friends who had attended, I learned that the fracas had started in the same row I would have been sitting in had I gone.

Another time I was listening to a girlfriend rave about a new man she had met and as she talked I blurted out, "He's married." This led to a big argument because I had never seen the man and was only saying what I felt as I listened to her description of him and the encounter they had had. I forgot about this incident until about a week later when my friend called me to say that she had checked out the man and found out he was married.

In the beginning I didn't talk about what I was doing with anyone. No one else in my circle ever talked about psychic powers and I didn't want to seem odd. But when I thought more about it, I remembered that when I was growing up my grandmother would often say things like, "Uh, oh, I've got a funny feeling about [something or other]" or "Cousin Eva was around me all night and she let me know I should [do this or that]." Her cousin Eva had died as a young girl decades before I was born.

Even so, I still wasn't comfortable talking about my feelings and instincts with others. Maybe my father influenced me. He had a habit of reacting to his mother's premonitions by saying, "There you go again, Mama, with that 'ole timey' mumbo jumbo. We modern folks don't go by all that stuff." I didn't want to be considered an "old-timer," so at first I simply kept my mouth shut about what I was doing.

But, after a few years, when I felt increasingly confident of my own powers, I started telling friends. I didn't feel that I was special or gifted in a way that others weren't. When I was asked for advice I would usually respond with, "Listen to your heart and follow your mind first."

Almost two years from that night in 1971, I decided to test my self-training by imagining a dress that I wanted for a party. I had always been plagued with having champagne taste and beer pockets, so I often had trouble finding an affordable dress that I liked. If anything I was doing had any meaning or power, such powers would surely guide me in small matters such as choosing a dress as well as important ones. So I decided that it would be fun to try my self-training on what was really a nonessential item.

As I got out of the car at the shopping mall and entered the store, I kept telling myself that I would be led to the right dress. It took a half hour to find the perfect dress, in the right size, and at a price I had in mind. I laughed at the fun! But, looking back years later, I point to this occasion as the time when I absolutely knew my self-training worked.

After that, day by day, week by week, month by month, and year by year, I continued to set a goal, pay attention to my instincts and gut feelings, follow that guidance, achieve the goal, and move on to the next one. I began to see myself differently too. No longer did I feel at the mercy of circumstance or fate. I began to realize that I could mold and shape circumstances to my own personal desires.

About the goals

My goals were wide ranging. Shortly after the successful dress-buying incident I began having trouble with a supervisor at work who did not seem to appreciate me. I respected her, but her lack of praise for the projects I thought I had done well hurt me. Resolving this matter became my next goal and I began to pay close attention to my interactions with her. I eventually realized that I was being thin-skinned in my reactions to her cut-and-dry acceptance of my completed assignments. Even though she was not effusive, she was always courteous.

I realized that my need to be praised was coming from my own lack of confidence. It was my own low self-esteem, not her manner, that was causing my discomfort. I began to be more careful about my work, and I learned to praise myself when I had completed my projects to the best of my ability. The more I congratulated myself, the more assured I was by the knowledge that my work had passed my own personal standards. And I did not find myself mentally asking her, "Well, what do you think, is it all right?" I got to the point where, when she did offer a compliment, it was like icing on the cake rather than something I had to have for my own well-being.

More goals

I got my first brand-new car about three years after I started my self-training. Despite all the Band-Aids my mechanic had applied to my rusty '55 Chevy, she had died. I had had it with car trouble, but buying a new car seemed like an impossible dream. So I spent some time taking the bus before my dream could be realized.

Not having credit was one stumbling block and I was determined not to ask my father to co-sign a car loan. After weeks of brooding about this goal, I mentioned to a coworker at the health center my desire for a new car. She said, "Didn't you hear? Our center has been made a part of the credit union for State employees. Why don't you apply for a loan from them?"

I contacted them and received an application form that seemed complicated with long pages of fine print. My first thought was that it was hopeless. But my instincts told me that if I took the time and read the application line by line I would be able to complete it correctly. I told myself not to become intimidated by the request for established credit information that I didn't have. I finished the form, answering all the questions as best I could. Then I had a flash that said, "Add a page explaining that even though you don't have credit, you're a good risk because of your steady employment and positive job evaluations." I did that and included a copy of my latest job performance report, which I also talked about with the loan officer when I returned the application in person. Following my instincts worked. I got the loan.

Relationship goals included

I used my pearls of wisdom for relationship goals as well. My sister and I used to fight a lot when we were in our twenties.

We were both strong willed, and we'd scream at each other until one of us would end up hanging up the phone on the other. We'd stay estranged for days at a time. Then I decided that our arguments were silly. Besides, we really liked each other's company. And my sister could make me laugh no matter what particular angst I was experiencing at the time.

So I set a goal of following my instincts that told me to hold my tongue and not pick fights with her. When she was bossy, I'd take a deep breath and count to ten before I responded. Or I would deliberately turn my mind to something funny she had said or some favor she had done for me. My efforts led to a much more harmonious relationship.

Help yourself

After twenty-five years, I am ready to tell you how to use the pearls of wisdom to achieve your goals, whether your goal is finding a husband or wife, finding a new job, or achieving professional success. If you are feeling a gnawing inside to be more, to achieve more, despite the fact that what you have is acceptable, I think my ten pearls can help you. If you have reached a certain point in your life where you have looked around and asked, "Is this it?" I think my ten pearls can help you.

The personal pearls of wisdom

To begin I want to give you the ten pearls along with a brief description of each one:

1. BELIEVE. To be successful you must, first of all, believe in yourself. You might want to get a better job, become a politician, fall in love, buy a sports car, or take a trip to Paris. Your belief that you can do whatever you set your mind to becomes the grain of sand that is the base of each pearl.

2. REMEMBER. This is the way to help yourself become a believer. Deliberately recall all your past achievements. Take a pencil and paper and write them down. The tangible presence of your achievements helps to strengthen your belief.

3. DECIDE. What specific goal do you want to work on first? Say to yourself, "I want to . . ."
4. PLAN. Plant the grain of sand in the oyster of your goal. Use each step in your plan like a layer of nacre that covers the grain of sand, one layer on top of another, until it becomes a lustrous, finished pearl.
5. ACTUATE. Go. Get off the dime. Move. Taking even the smallest, seemingly insignificant steps toward your goal will launch your dreams.
6. HABITUATE. Make the use of the pearls a habit by taking at least one action on your plan each day. Never let the sun go down without having done at least one thing, no matter how small, toward your goal.
7. PRETEND. This is the fun step. At least once a day, playact. Imagine how you will be when you achieve your goal.
8. REFINE. In this step, using the image you have of yourself at your goal, you smooth out any bumps, hitches, or nicks that may be in that picture, before you reach the goal.

9. CLAIM. This is the hardest step to realize. I say this because we get so used to our daily circumstances, it is hard for us to think, "I, little ole me, can actually be ... (the boss, a movie star, happily married ...)." This pearl focuses on acquiring the feeling of deserving success.

10. EXPAND. After achieving your small dreams, let your mind soar and move on to bigger and better goals.

Fifteen minutes of concentration

Now read this book to the end. Then go back to the beginning and start to work on the pearls. How do you work on the pearls? Each and every day spend fifteen minutes concentrating on the ten pearls, fifteen minutes on all ten pearls combined. While concentrating, listen to your heart. This means noting any hunches that might come to you, pinpointing any gut feelings that you may have at the time. You can write down your feelings if you want. It's easier that way, at least at the start.

At first you may feel this exercise is silly. I did. But then I thought that feeling silly didn't matter because I believed that what I was doing was going to be of help to me. I still do.

You can have Paris

Let me tell you a story. One of my friends had had for many years a fantasy of someday taking a trip to Paris. After I told her about what I was doing with the ten pearls, she made up her mind to use them to make her dream come true.

Every day she thought about the trip and mentally worked to strengthen her belief that it would materialize. She was starting from scratch in that she had not saved a lot of money. She began to read any articles or books about Paris that she could find. The more she increased her knowledge about the city, the stronger her belief that she could get there became.

She wrote down the ten pearls and each morning she looked over her notes. She would start to concentrate by saying, "I believe that I will get to Paris." To help herself believe that she could get something that seemed impossible for her, she consciously began to remember other goals she had achieved over the years. Recalling that she had achieved those seemingly impossible goals gave her confidence in herself.

She decided to formalize her goal by telling all her friends about it. "I'm going to Paris this year or never."

Then she started to plan for the trip. She got information on airlines schedules and tour packages. At work she inquired about how she could combine vacation time with leave time so that her job would be waiting when she returned. Every day she took some kind of action toward her goal, even if it was just flipping through one of the picture books of Paris that she kept at her office and at home. Concentrating on Paris became a habit with her.

She told me that every day she also spent a few minutes fantasizing about her visit. She'd think to herself, "I'm in Paris now," and then she'd imagine herself riding on the Metro, visiting Notre Dame, and having delicious dinners at charming and inexpensive little restaurants on the Left Bank.

Finally, as she put it, she began to "get down to business"

with her plans. She scraped together money to cover the plane ticket, food, and incidental expenses but she didn't have enough for the cost of a hotel. She thought about staying at a youth hostel, but decided that she was too mature to be able to enjoy the dormitory-style accommodations. She acknowledged to her friends that she was in a quandary about this but, at the same time, she reiterated her determination to achieve her goal. In fact, every time she had a conversation with friends, she talked about her trip and the current status of her plans.

Of course, not everyone was encouraging. Sometimes the reaction would be, "Oh, girl, forget it. So you don't go to Paris? So what?" She didn't let those kinds of remarks discourage her, however. Her belief was so strong that she'd usually retort with something like, "I am going. I deserve to go." It was always all in good humor, but her responses reflected the fact that in her mind she had claimed her right to achieve her dream.

Time passed and one day she was having lunch with an acquaintance whom she hadn't seen for some time. During the course of their conversation she brought up her Paris plans, and the other woman mentioned that her nephew was a journalist who lived in Paris. "But he has to come back to the States for two months and he's having trouble finding someone to house-sit his Paris apartment," she went on to say. My friend reports that she instantly had a flash that told her to offer to house-sit for the nephew. She said that she hesitated for about one minute, because she didn't know the woman that well and thought the woman would think she was being forward. But she followed her flash anyway.

"Well, next time I talk to him, I'll tell him about you," the woman replied. Two weeks later my friend got a call from the journalist. One thing led to another and in a short time she was ensconced in Paris, pinching herself and having the time of her life.

She is convinced that the realization of her long-held dream came about because she used the ten pearls of wisdom. She believed in her dream and she fortified that belief through remembering her past accomplishments. She made a definite decision of "this year or never." She actuated her steps toward her goal on a daily basis. By taking at least one daily step she made actuating a habit. She spent some time playacting and pretending that she was in Paris. She claimed her dream by convincing herself that she had a right to it. She refined her plans and heeded the flash that led to removing the "bump" of not having a place to stay. And, when she got to Paris, she expanded her dream by making contacts and developing relationships that have now led to her being able to go back to Paris for at least a month every year.

Heed your flashes

Tune in and take note of the flashes and instincts that come to you during your daily fifteen minutes of concentration. I'm using the word *flash* to describe those thoughts, gut feelings, and perceptions that come to us unexpectedly and at great speed. No matter how silly or seemingly impossible they may appear to you, always pay attention to them. Use a journal to record your flashes. Take it out at the end of the day and read it; this reminds you to follow through. A journal does not have to be fancy. My daily journal, if I wanted to call it that, is a little three-by-five-inch spiral notepad I bought at the local supermarket.

I promise you that the actions you take on these flashes and gut feelings will lead you to your goals. Remember: Tune in and take note. Write them down. And, most important, act on them. Those flashes are highly personal. They are *your* guides and *your* guides alone, as they come from your own heart.

How to work it

This morning, as I do every morning, I woke up, looked at the clock, and started my fifteen minutes of concentration by reviewing my ten pearls of wisdom. When you start to do this, you might want to keep a copy of the list on a pad next to your bed. Then when you wake up, you can check off the pearls as you finish thinking about them.

If you don't want to do this as soon as you wake up, you can concentrate while you shower, comb your hair, or brush your teeth. If this seems far-fetched to you, try to remember what you thought about today after waking up and while grooming. I'm willing to bet it was about some problem you may be having. If that's so, why not change that and spend the time concentrating on the ten pearls for your own success?

It's up to you to select a fifteen minute period of the day that works for you. Selecting and adhering to your private fifteen minutes per day will become easier as you practice using the pearls. You will finally reach a point where if you skip a day for any reason you will feel out of kilter. That's good. You want using your pearls to become second nature, and those feelings can keep you on track as you work toward your goals.

Keep at it

I recommend that you try using the ten pearls for one month. To begin, choose a goal that is relatively unimportant and try the pearls on it. When you attain that goal — and you will — choose another. You will gain confidence as you move from smaller goals to more important ones. Continued practice will strengthen your foundation and allow the pearls to work for you.

The ten pearls worked for me, allowing me to become successful and to achieve goal after goal after goal for the past twenty-five years. Some of those goals were on a large scale like getting a master's degree and a great job right away. Other goals were smaller, like winning a coveted part in an amateur theater production, or even finding the perfect parking space at a specific time. But every goal was important enough for me to spend a concentrated fifteen minutes per day with my pearls of wisdom.

Bought sense

I know that by now you might be thinking that I am crazy, and this is not how you can achieve your goals. As my grandmother used to say, "There is bought sense and there is borrowed sense." What she meant was this: There is knowledge that we obtain in life from actually experiencing situations for ourselves. We go through events and we take out information from these events that we make our own. Then we use this information to guide us as we proceed in life. That is bought sense. We bought and paid for that knowledge and the wisdom that results from that knowledge through the trials and tribulations we went through to get it.

Borrowed sense, on the other hand, is information that we have gained from others. Other people experience events and get information from those occasions. Then they tell us about them and impart the wisdom they have gleaned. We can use this wisdom as we go along in life and sometimes it helps us.

The pearls of wisdom I am describing in this book are bought sense for me. I experienced what I am writing about and I know that the pearls work. Right now, for you, the information is borrowed sense. That's okay for now. You will buy it soon enough.

In each of the following chapters I will describe one pearl of the strand and provide some background to clarify what is involved. Then I will give examples of the actions I took in order to implement that particular pearl. I will also suggest some actions that you might want to take.

Through reading and taking actions as you go along, you will begin to experience the sense of surety and confidence that will lead you to achieve your personal goals. These experiences will make the pearls of wisdom become bought sense for you. For now, as you read the book, take it on faith that this borrowed sense contains something of positive value.

Go slowly, at your own pace. You don't have to rush. Nobody is timing you. But whatever you do, start now.

The Pearl *of* BELIEVE

Faith, absolute dogmatic faith, is the only law of true success.
—Ralph Waldo Trine

Cultivating the pearls

To be successful—to achieve a goal—you must, first of all, believe that it is possible to do so. We have all heard this many times. When we hear it we often react with skepticism. But acceptance and mastery of this axiom is crucial if the strand of pearls of wisdom is to work. Belief is the core grain of sand for each pearl. Your belief in any endeavor is your first step. My grandmother used to say, "Every tub has to stand on its own bottom." She meant that any accomplishment had to have its own solid foundation. You must lay a solid foundation for all your goals and that solid bedrock is belief.

Smidgen of disbelief

I remember hearing a story, one that I'm sure has been told for centuries, but it illustrates a point about belief.

The story is about a woman who had a mountain in front of her door that prevented her from going very far. Any kind of venturing out of her house turned into a major hardship because of this mountain. The woman liked to think that she was a woman of faith, that she was a believer. So she decided to pray.

One day, she got down on her knees and prayed and prayed. She poured her heart out to her God.

"Please remove this mountain from in front of my door," she beseeched, with her eyes tightly closed and her hands folded reverently in front of her.

Finally, after almost a whole day spent on her knees in prayer, she got up and looked out of the door.

The mountain was still there.

The woman shook her head and said out loud, "I knew it."

The point of the story is the fact that to believe, to be a believer, you have to do just that. You have to believe, totally, without a doubt. Even though the woman in the story probably thought she was a believer, she was not. She hedged her bet. She had doubt about her prayer. The statement "I knew it" revealed that, in her heart, she did not really believe that her prayer could move that mountain.

My experience with using the ten pearls of wisdom has taught me that without a doubt belief is absolutely pivotal. The effectiveness of all the other pearls hinges on this one. You can't hold back a little smidgen of disbelief. You can't be on the safe side.

The past can help

There are simple exercises that you can do to help you become a believer.

Let's go back to your childhood, your grade school days. Let's recall a friend or classmate who always seemed to excel in any endeavor that he or she undertook. There was certainly a Jenine, or a Beth, or a Rodney in your class who got the highest marks, who won the awards at the end of the school year, a boy or girl who was the favorite of the teachers and the principal. Remember those children and their successes.

Can you recall any trait that they seemed to demonstrate at all times? Weren't they always the first ones to say, "I can. . . . I will. . . . I know that."? Whether it was tackling a math problem or trying out for the lead in the school play, their responses reflected a can-do attitude and a confident belief in their own abilities.

If you read the biographies of successful people, there is an underlying theme to many of them. They all, consciously or unconsciously, believed that they would achieve what they set out to do.

Building belief

The ability to believe without a doubt is the basic foundation of the pearls of wisdom. So it is well worth the time and effort it takes to train yourself to be a believer. In order to train yourself, try the methods below for two or three days in a row.

1. *Sit down in a quiet place where you will not be disturbed and think about the people you know who are successful.*
   I'm not talking about celebrities. They could be people whom you actually know and who are successful *by your own personal standards,* whatever those may be. They could be people like your friend Jeff, who just got a promotion; your sister, Mattie, a divorced mother who has raised three children who have all turned out well; your airhead cousin, Tillie, who has made a profit the first year operating a yogurt stand in the shopping mall.

   These should be people like you, whom you know and identify with.

   I have a friend who comes to mind. She is a respected teacher. Because of her delightful personality and her constant willingness to help others she is well-liked. At the same time she is an accomplished artist and has been one since her childhood. Just sharing a lunchtime conversation with her is like hearing an art lecture. Drawing from her

rich cultural heritage she devises her own art pieces —
paintings on canvas, little altars and shrines, jewelry,
figurines of saints, ceremonial masks. She instills them with
a dynamic quality that is beautiful and irresistible.

Many times she creates pieces and gives them as gifts. She
loves teaching but, at the same time, she identifies herself as
an artist. She believes in her soul that art is her calling. It is
clear that that belief in herself as an artist comes from her heart.

Her belief has certainly brought her success. Recently
she received an award from one of the most prestigious
foundations in the country. It was a total surprise because
the nominations for this award are anonymous. The candi-
dates do not know that they are being considered until the
selection is final. The award comes with a fellowship that is
equivalent to three years of the recipient's salary. This fellowship allows the recipient to take off from paid employment for three years to devote their energy to their creative
calling without having to worry about meeting their daily

expenses. My friend is now able to develop and expand her art in freedom.

I am convinced that this joyful occurrence in her life came about because of her unshakable belief in herself as an artist. But even before she received her award, she was one of my favorite personal role models.

2. *After you have chosen your individuals, think about the kind of personality they have. Think about what they say when they talk, including any pet phrases they may use.* Jeff probably talked often about the good ideas he had for running the department better or how he would do things more efficiently if he was in a supervisory position. Mattie probably has the habit of talking about how much faith she had that her children would turn out okay and how, even when things got tough, the family pulled together. Airhead Tillie probably bubbled about her yogurt stand idea well in advance of opening it up.

3. *As you do this exercise you will realize that all of these people have a common theme that runs through their personalities.* It is the theme of belief. They all, in one way or the other, manifest that they are believers and they demonstrate a can-do attitude.

   These are everyday, average, normal people whom you know, who are nonetheless people who have achieved their goals. They may not be continually successful in everything they do all the time. But they have succeeded with regard to specific, stated goals they have set for themselves.

4. *For the last part of the exercise think about people who are considered by the world to be successful.* These will not be the Jeffs, the Matties, and the Tillies that you know but will be people who are written up in the newspapers, magazines, and books.

   Go to the bookstore or library to get one or two biographies of successful people. As you read them you will become

aware of the theme of belief that has permeated the lives of
all these individuals. You will recognize the theme of belief,
and you will recognize that these people manifested a can-do
attitude, usually at a young age.

It may be that the individual did not consciously recognize
this attitude in themselves. But read what other people have
to say about them. There will be statements like "As a child
she was different, always so determined" or "I knew Johnny
was going to be successful. Whatever we did, he was always
the leader." These statements reflect that the basic trait of
belief was dominant.

Doubting is easy

To be a doubter is easy, it comes naturally to a lot of us. At the same
time, to be a believer can also be just as easy. It can come just as naturally. If this were not the case, civilization would not have come
as far as it has. For humans to have progressed at all, individuals
had to have believed in something better than what they had.

Do it for yourself

For the next few days, concentrate on training yourself to be a believer. Do the exercise suggested on pages 33 to 36. Concentrate on your own thoughts and listen to yourself speak. Do you use the pet phrase, "I don't believe it"? If so, stop saying that.

Responding with disbelief may seem unimportant, but this habit can erode of your ability to maintain a positive outlook. Focus on going through your days with an expectant attitude regarding even the smallest positives. When you catch yourself doubting, stop the thought process and consciously turn the doubt statement around. Instead of saying "Oh, yeah?" Concentrate on saying "Hmmmm, maybe." Don't go to the bank *expecting* to have to wait in a long line. *Expect* to get there at just the right time when there is no line. Instead of *expecting* that the cleaner is not going to be able to get that stain out of your brand-new silk blouse, *expect* that the blouse will be cleaned perfectly. Dissolve any disbelief, even in the smallest, most insignificant instance.

If you are a doubter, you have to consciously train yourself to be a believer. I want you to start today. As in most of our endeavors, all it takes is practice to become proficient in doing it well. I want you to start to practice being a believer.

First things first

You have to work on yourself in order to recognize the usefulness of the pearl of believe. Belief has to become your first reaction and in that way it pervades all of your thoughts and activities. Only then do you begin to approach your dreams with the expectation that they will be realized in your life.

We often spend as much time worrying about our status as losers instead of consolidating our status as winners. Both states rest on the mental building blocks we have used to set our foundation. Determine to have your foundation based on your strong sense of belief in yourself and your ability to get what you want out of life.

The ABCs — how to work it

A. PLUNGE INTO THE USE OF THE PEARL OF BELIEVE. Just do it! Tell yourself that you are going to stop thinking negatively about events. Tell yourself that instead you are going to think and feel positively about all you undertake. Forget Murphy's Law. Let it work for other people, but decide that it is not going to work for you. Make your own law and let it be something like "If anything can go right, it will." Convince yourself that what you think and say about the world is just as important as what Murphy thought or said. Who was Murphy anyway? You don't even know. So why is his law any better than your own?

B. NO ONE CAN REALLY KNOW WHAT IS GOING ON IN YOUR MIND. Isn't that wonderful? So you can think any kind of thoughts that you want. Let them be thoughts that lift you and cheer you and encourage you. You are your own biggest fan. And you have a lot of time alone with your thoughts. Combine those two factors and make good use of them to help you become a believer. Fans are loyal. Fans wouldn't spend time telling themselves their heroine can't sing or their hero can't dance. Fans see their heroine or hero and most of the things that person does in a positive light. Become such a fan of yourself that you begin to see yourself and what you do in a positive light. Train yourself.

C. BE YOUR OWN EXPERT. No one knows you better than you know yourself. You are an authority on you. Accept that and allow it to grow and become strong within your mind. Build that strength. Say to yourself that, when all is said and done, you are the authority when it comes to how you see the world. And you can decide what your perception of the world is going to be. Let that authority become your baseline in everything you think and do.

The Pearl *of* REMEMBER

What you follow... follows you.
—Eleanor Brooks Johnson

The value of memory

When I awake in the morning, I immediately focus on my pearls of wisdom and my list of goals. During this time I always include some thoughts about past successes. Recalling your own achievements can help you see yourself as a winner, someone who can achieve goals rather than someone who just dreams of them. It's easy to get defeated when thinking about your dreams. They may seem impossibly distant. Remembering things that you have accomplished can pull you away from dreary thinking.

One of the ways to view yourself as an achiever is to consciously go back in your memory to times in the past when you accomplished something that you set out to do. My grandmother used to get us to do this when we were growing up. One time I was agonizing about a final exam in biology, worrying that I wouldn't get a good grade even though I had studied hard. She said, "You felt the same way last year when your algebra final came up. Remember that? You were so worried even though you had studied. And you ended up getting an A. Think about that. It'll help you stop worrying now." Then she added a favorite phrase of hers, "What you follow, follows you."

These words of encouragement became a beacon for us and let us imagine some new success around the corner.

I have a friend who has perfected the pearl of remember in a beautiful way. She has made a collage of photos from her past that were taken at events in her life that she considers examples of her successes. She has had it framed and it hangs in her bedroom. The photos include:

- her graduation from grade school
- her award-winning high school debate team

- her high school graduation
- her first car
- she and the love of her life on a trip to the Bahamas
- the first photo of her daughter
- a group photo taken at an awards ceremony where she was crowned "Businesswoman of the Year" by her professional colleagues
- a group photo taken on a wilderness trip when she reached the top of a mountain she'd thought she'd never be able to climb

The collage contains these and a few other photos that remind her of milestones she has achieved in her life. It is a constant inspiration to her.

The picture that works for me

There is one success in my life that has evolved as the picture that always encourages me no matter how impossible any of my current goals seem. That is the experience of going back to school and getting my degrees. Whenever I find myself feeling daunted by something I am dealing with and feeling like I'm hitting a brick wall, I make myself remember that process.

I was in my late twenties and going back to college took tremendous effort. I was tired of my work as a clerk, but I knew I would have to continue that at least while I pursued my studies. I didn't have money saved and I didn't have a scholarship. I had to learn to research and fill out grant applications. I had to change my shift at work so that I could go to school days and work nights. Most of my friends didn't understand what I was doing and why, and many were not very supportive. I had no social life to speak of and was very lonely at times.

But despite all of this I persevered. Then, in my last year of college, I learned that I needed a master's degree to get the kind of job I wanted in the field I had chosen. So I started applying to graduate school. I was accepted. I entered graduate school, finished, was handed my master's degree, and was launched on a new career path.

I'm presenting that story in a succinct manner but I can assure you that everything else I have encountered and achieved seems small alongside the long hard grind of higher education. It was hard and to minimize how hard it was would defeat the purpose of recalling those years. Precisely because it was so hard and because I got through it, that time in my life is the touchstone I use to prepare myself when I take on any new goal, however monumental.

You have been successful

What you need to do is to go back in your mind and remember some activity that you set out to accomplish and that you were successful in achieving. Think about the steps you took in the process. As accurately as you can, recall your thoughts and feelings when the going got tough. Remember what it was that pulled you through. And, most important, remember how you felt when you arrived at the goal. There is nothing like that feeling, is there? How good you felt. How you smiled. How proud you were when you received the congratulations of others. Or, if no one else knew about it, how proud *you* felt.

The beauty of this pearl

Nothing teaches us better than our own experiences. Remember my grandmother's bought sense and borrowed sense? No one can really push you to be successful. The drive has to come from within. That's why I'm urging you to comb your memory and recall your own accomplishments. This is your very own bought sense that you can draw from as you continue forward to your goals, buying more sense as you go along.

Recalling the success of others can certainly inspire us. Reading about Oprah, how she started out poor and disadvantaged and is now a millionaire beloved by countless fans is inspiring to me. Or hearing about how Joe Montana started at the bottom of the draft pick and went on to become an acclaimed figure in sports history gives all of us encouragement.

Still, ultimately, nothing inspires me like using the pearl of remember to focus on something *I did*.

I'm convinced that using this step is an excellent way to solidify your own foundation for success. If you try *remembering* on a daily basis, you will help yourself stay on the road to your goal.

The ABCs — how to work it

A. YOU ARE AN ACHIEVER. You've lived some life already. You've grown up. You've gotten a job at some point. You've fallen in love. Maybe you have children. You've made friends. You have a hobby that absorbs you. So you see, you are already pretty special. Your circle may be small and you may not have had the proverbial fifteen minutes of fame, but you've got a life. You've already attained and passed through some pretty significant milestones. On a daily basis, review those. Keep them in mind as you go about your day. And if you never go any further than you are right now, know that you already have accomplishments under your belt.

B. ON A DAILY BASIS, MENTALLY REVIEW WHAT YOU HAVE
    ALREADY ACCOMPLISHED. Think about it often and men-
    tally pat yourself on the back. I saw a best-selling author
    being interviewed on television once. On being asked how
    he felt about all the accolades that were coming to him, he
    replied, "Yes, it's all wonderful. But I happen to think that
    if I get up in the morning and get through the day doing
    some work, having a few laughs with my wife and kids,
    and then relaxing around a couple of beers with a few
    friends, then I've done well. If that's all I do that day, I'm
    satisfied." Here was someone who had dazzled thousands
    but, at the same time, he basically saw himself as successful
    because of those achievements in his life that some people
    would call small potatoes.

C. TEACH YOURSELF TO LUXURIATE IN YOUR OWN,
    SO-CALLED, SMALL-SCALE ACHIEVEMENTS. Recall them
    often and let those thoughts circulate in your mind. Relax

into those thoughts and let them help you see that you are already an achiever. Growing this mental image of yourself as someone who is already solid, steady, and getting along pretty well will be invaluable to you as you work toward attaining your goals and dreams.

The Pearl *of* DECIDE

If the thing you wish to do is right, and you believe in it, *go ahead and do it!*
—Napoleon Hill

Make up your mind

*I*n order to be successful—to achieve a goal—you have to decide on one. To do anything you have to, first of all, decide to do it. There has to be a definite mental action of deciding that this is what you want to do.

Do you watch television shows on which celebrities appear or do you read magazines that have stories about celebrities? Do you remember a statement that many of these people make? It's usually something like "When I was five, I decided to be an actress" or "Since I was twelve I have wanted to run my own business" or "I decided to race cars when I was eight." Isn't it so that most people who have made it big in one way or another can designate a point in time when they made a conscious decision to do whatever it is that they are considered successful at?

With regard to the past, history is replete with stories of people who made decisions and acted on them. Go back and read their stories and let them inspire you to come to a decision in your life. Harriet Tubman made a decision to risk her own life to help others to freedom. John H. Johnson, the founder of *Ebony*, made a decision to put out a magazine aimed entirely at an audience that few advertisers had even acknowledged existed, and then built that magazine into a glorious publishing empire.

I know a former police chief who became the mayor against all odds. And when I say all odds, I mean all odds. His announcement was greeted with derision by most of the political pundits in town. The so-called experts wrote him off, even up to the last few days before the election. He won though. And after about two tumultuous years in office, I happened to be present when a reporter asked him what had sustained him through the effort. He told the reporter that one day he had decided that he would run for mayor and try to do all he could for the city where he had been born. He said that he had decided to do it, and that he had decided to let nothing stop him.

It was the same with a venerable professor who was quite elderly by the time I knew him. He had been a victim of polio as a child and the condition had confined him to a wheelchair for the better part of his life. He recounted how, when he had applied for graduate school at a major eastern university, he had been denied entrance because the admissions committee thought that his being in a wheelchair in the classroom would distract the other students. This was long before the days of the Americans With Disabilities Act. But he persisted and eventually he did gain admission. He went on to achieve a long and illustrious career in the academic world. I asked him how it all had happened. He said that he had decided on what he wanted and he had also decided not to let any obstacles stand in his way.

Taking the plunge

Sometimes there is a long process in the evolution of a decision. Dr. Wayne W. Dyer in his book *You'll See It When You Believe It,* provides a marvelous description of the evolution of a major decision he made in his life:

> *Though I loved teaching at the university, something inside of me said that I needed to go off on my own, needed to shift gears and go in an entirely new direction.... I struggled for almost a year with the idea that I had to go out on my own and leave the security of a bimonthly paycheck.... I had wonderful pictures in my mind's eye. I saw myself talking to everyone in America about the ideas I had just finished writing about...The morning came when the picture was very clear in my mind.... I knew that this was the day, that within a few hours I would officially be out on my own, no longer able to rely on a paycheck.*

To me this is one of the most eloquent descriptions of a process of making a decision I have read. Despite all the misgivings and trepidation he may have had, Dr. Dyer *made a decision.* And, as it has turned out, the decision was the right one for him. He has gone on to become a best-selling author and lecturer, known worldwide for his books and teachings.

I give these examples to highlight the essence of this pearl of *decide,* to show that you must have a definite starting point on the road to any goal. If you search your own mind, I am sure you will be able to remember a day, or an hour, when you finally decided to apply for your job, to make that first date, to commit your energy to perfecting some skill.

One woman I know decided that she wanted to make some extra income and thought for a long time how she could go about doing it and keep her day job. She then decided to sell arts and crafts at fairs and flea markets. Although she was not an artist or craftsman, she had a love for such objects and often bought them, and knew that a lot of others did as well.

She started going to garage sales and auctions, picking up items that she liked at bargain prices. Then she would polish them up and sell them at stands she would reserve at the local fairs. She was so successful that she saved up enough money to go on a trip to Alaska where she found other items, brought them back, and sold them. What had started out as a personal enthusiasm, soon became not only a source of income—but an activity that gave her a lot of satisfaction.

Eventually she earned a reputation for having a discerning eye for unique items. Some of her customers told her about specific things they wanted, asking her to keep a look out for them. She was successful doing that. Now she is in a position to take at least two major trips per year. She travels around the country both as a tourist and as an agent for her customers. This is all in her spare time, as she never left the job that she loves. All this comes from taking that first step.

How I see you

I will make some assumptions here. I am assuming that you probably have a life that is more or less okay. You probably have a job, a way to support yourself. And if worse came to worse you could probably maintain your current status for years and still be okay. However, even though things are okay, I am assuming that you have some recurring thoughts that things could be better for you. I assume that you sometimes think that your relationship with your mate could be more satisfying or that your family life could be happier.

Or it could be that you think that you would be much more attractive if you lost thirty pounds. Maybe you think that if you were the boss you could run your company better and make bigger profits. You could be thinking that if you broke into the entertainment business, you have what it takes to be a star. Maybe your idea is that, if you got your degree, you could be a great biology teacher.

Something is there, and I have no real way of knowing exactly what it is for you. But I am assuming something is there in the back of your mind that made you want to know more about how to achieve your goals. This is the something that made you buy this book and read it, or accept it from a friend and read it.

If my assumptions have any truth to them, then I can tell you that whatever your personal situation is, it is up to you to decide what you are going to do about it. It is up to you to decide how you want things to be different.

The nitty gritty

Take a pencil and paper and do some jotting as you think about yourself. What attracted you to this book? What is the goal that you want to achieve and the dream that you want to capture? It's got to be there or you wouldn't be looking at this page.

What is it? Pinpoint your goal. Write it on a piece of paper, scratch it out, and write it out again. Keep doing this until you come up with goals that are clear to you. Then make a decision. It's not up to your mate, or your children, or your father. It's up to you to decide what your goal or dream will be. And, until you do that, you can't work on achieving it.

For a lot of people this simple task is hard to do. Some will never do it. They will waste years complaining about their state in life and they don't realize that until they make *decisions on definite goals,* nothing is going to change for them. They will continue to tread water rather than swim the distance.

We all know people like this. You know them and I know them. You'll ask them how they are and they will respond with some statement about how their life is the same old way. They usually add a sigh. We've all met people who react to life like that. And that's all right—for them.

You are different

That's not for you, of course. You want your life to be different than it is and better than it is according to your personal desires. You've certainly made that decision. And you have decided to read a book that will help you achieve your goals. So you've already taken steps.

I truly believe that all goals, as long as they are not violating someone else, are attainable. Violating others means deliberately abusing someone else in order to obtain your objectives. Let's say that your goal is to obtain a supervisory position at your job. In order to achieve that goal you try to impress your boss by taking credit for work that you did not do or you tell lies and undercut the reputation of others in order to make yourself look good. That's violation. These methods do not work. You may get the job you're after but somehow, in some way, you will not gain satisfaction. You may be exposed and everyone will know that you have lied. Or if you have not really laid solid groundwork and fully prepared yourself to do the work in the new position, you may make mistakes and eventually lose the job.

Even if you avert catastrophe and you keep the new position for years, your own guilt could get the best of you by making you tense in constant anticipation of being revealed as incompetent or untrustworthy.

The bottom line is that achieving goals by deliberately abusing someone else is ultimately not worth it. The old saying about reaping what you sow is still operative. My grandmother used to put it another way. She would say, "When you dig a ditch for someone else, you had better dig two ditches. You're going to need one for yourself."

But if your goals and dreams are not abusing others, then decide to pursue them. Decide what your goals for yourself are going to be. Decide on your goals and get on with them.

The ABCs — how to work it

A. WHAT WERE YOUR THOUGHTS WHEN YOU PICKED UP THIS BOOK? What attracted you to it? If someone else gave it to you, why did you take it, open it, and start to read it? Stop right now and answer this question for yourself. Mull over your answer. You want something in your life to be different. Things are pretty good, but you think they could be better in some way.

ℬ. WHAT IS THAT SPECIFIC WAY? ARE YOU CLEAR ABOUT IT IN YOUR OWN MIND? Can you explain to yourself, out loud, exactly what it is about your life that you want to be different? Keep thinking about it until you can recite to yourself, out loud, what it is. It may take some time to determine the specifics, but take that time.

𝒞. NOW THAT YOU HAVE WHAT YOU WANT TO DO CLEAR IN YOUR MIND, ASK YOURSELF, WHAT'S KEEPING YOU FROM DOING IT? What is holding you back? Who is holding you back? Does that person have more to say about what you do with your life than you do? I don't think so. And, I'll bet, you don't think so either, not really. Go ahead. Make your decision.

The Pearl *of* PLAN

Life became simple again…Freda had planned it like that.
—From the novel *Mama* by Terry McMillan

Dream making

*N*ow that you have decided on your goal or goals, you have to make your plan. A plan is a step-by-step outline of a particular course of action. This outline will involve countless small and seemingly ineffectual steps but, like the layer upon layer of nacre that coats the grain of sand in the heart of the oyster, your adherence to your plan will produce that most lustrous of pearls, your dream come true.

Planning is the given in any successful endeavor. Napoleon Hill, in the book *Think & Grow Rich*, put it this way:

Everything man creates or acquires begins in the form of desire, that desire is taken on the first lap of its journey, from the

abstract to the concrete, into the workshop of the imagination,
where plans for its transition are created and organized.

Some notable planners

One of my favorite novelists is Terry McMillan. I like her books because her stories reflect life today and her characters are so real and recognizable to me.

In an article I read about her a few years ago, she described how hard she had worked on the task of getting the word out about her first novel. Not satisfied with her publisher's efforts, she devised her own plan to obtain the publicity that was necessary. She did research and learned about various colleges, book stores, and other forums that she felt would have an interest in her work. Then she proceeded to write to them and offered to do readings. She traveled all over the country. And her efforts paid off. Today her work is known and enjoyed by hundreds of thousands of people. Terry McMillan knew the importance of a specific, formalized plan and the importance of executing it to the smallest detail.

Most successful achievers start with a plan. Many members of Congress planned the progress of their political careers, starting with getting elected to the local school board, then to their town council, then to the state legislature, then on to Washington, D.C. Famous attorneys have started as law clerks, famous bridge builders started as draftsmen. From humble beginnings they have progressed, step by step, to the highest reaches of their profession. Each had a plan tailored to get them where they wanted to go.

David Packard, in his book *The HP Way,* talks about how, in the 1930's, he, Bill Hewlett, and a few of their friends were directed by one of their teachers to visit the firms in the San Francisco Bay Area that were concentrating on radio engineering and other types of technology. These visits were inspirational to the young men and, Packard says, "With Terman's encouragement, Bill Hewlett, Ed Porter, Barney Oliver, and I were making tentative plans to try to do something on our own after graduation." Time passed and, as Packard goes on to say,

"We started putting our plans to work. Bill had found a two-story house on Addison Avenue in Palo Alto, and Lu [Packard's wife] and I rented the lower floor. Bill, who at the time was still a bachelor, lived in a little building out back. There was also a one-car garage, and that became our workshop."

That one-car garage workshop was where they began to implement their plans. Those plans led to what is now one of the largest technology corporations in the world—Hewlett Packard.

Planning is absolutely essential

Most plans begin with a desire or a yearning to have some element of life be different. My career path started with my yearning to become a social worker. I worked with people who did social work and I admired them. At first I was a clerk. But observing what the social workers did encouraged me to explore the field. Realizing that the work involved helping people improve their lives was appealing to me and I started my plan to complete my education and become a social worker. It was a step-by-step process, not scattershot in any way, that I had to research and organize. Then, despite setbacks and roadblocks, I had to implement the steps and stick with that implementation.

Starting at square one

I have a relative who was a young single mother. She seemed to drift through life working at a succession of menial jobs. An intelligent woman, she yearned for a more fulfilling existence. Through her church she was on a committee of members who visited people who were ill, both in the hospital and at home. As time passed she realized that her volunteer work really meant a lot to her. She enjoyed it and it gave her a lot of satisfaction. Inspired by these feelings she decided that she wanted to be a nurse.

Following through on that decision, she made her plans to go into a nursing program that was offered at the community college. It was hard work for her to change her life, given her circumstances, but she made her plan and stuck with it. Finally she finished the program and got a job at a large hospital.

She worked for some time and then, growing restless, she decided she wanted to move to another city across the country. She didn't have much money, but she was determined. With that decision made, she started buying the newspaper from her chosen city and looking at the ads for nursing jobs. She followed up on the ads that appealed to her by sending her résumé. Then she made calls following up on the résumés. This resulted in four firm interviews.

But she had to get to the city to go to the interviews. Without the money for airfare, she decided to drive.

Moving on up

And so she began to plan her trip. She scheduled the interviews far enough in advance so that she could drive and arrive on time. Getting out the road maps, she plotted her itinerary and knew that she would have to make four overnight stops because she was driving alone. Calling the Chambers of Commerce in each city where she'd spend the night, she got information about safe and inexpensive motels. She contacted them and made her reservations.

In the end she got to the target city, went to the interviews, and was offered jobs at two of the four possibilities. She chose one, set the date to begin work, drove home, and started her plan for the actual move. As a result of her careful planning and persistent—and I mean persistent—follow-through on each step of her plan, she's now living a happy and productive life in a city she loves.

Making something happen

Plans do not evolve overnight. It takes time to think through what you want to do, research what it takes to do it, and then follow through on your research. Sometimes it will seem that you take two steps forward only to end up four steps behind. That is where your formal plan can help. You have something to look at, a road map, that lets you imagine the final product and gives you the strength of vision to plow through the brick walls.

Many times having a formal plan helps you articulate your dreams to others and get help from people such as family members or friends. By sharing her plans with her family, my relative was able to find child care while she went on her job interview trip. Or the help can come from people that you meet as you move along your path. While I was going to school I got invaluable encouragement from my fellow students, many of them younger than I was, and from my teachers.

Look around you. Most of what you see, whether it's a building or a small fruit and vegetable stand, has come into being because someone has taken the trouble to work out a step-by-step plan. When I get tired, or lazy, or discouraged about planning, I take a drive and spend time looking at the magnificent Golden Gate Bridge. It always revives me to realize that that marvelous structure was once deemed impossible to build. And yet there it stands, the result of a meticulous and brilliant plan. After years of study, the bridge was erected pillar by pile.

Planning counts with feelings too

So far I have focused on goals that target professional or career success. But your goals can also include emotional or psychological satisfaction. A concrete plan, a definite blueprint, is needed to reach these goals as well.

Let's say that your goal is to have a more harmonious home life. Is there constant arguing and confusion in your home between you and your mate or between you and your children?

Your planning can go something like this:

1. *Take some time alone in a quiet place and think about your situation.*

2. *Go over that argument you had this morning with your teenager about doing his homework.*

3. *Take a pencil and paper and write out everything that happened.* For example: "I said, 'I know you didn't do your homework last night. Even though I went to bed early I could hear you on the phone until after ten.' He said,

'But, Mom, I had had a hard day at school starting with that 6:30 A.M. weight-training class for football. I was tired.' "

4. *Relive the incident in your mind and use your notes to role play each part.* As you visualize each action and interaction, change your words to those that you wish you had used.

5. *See yourself engaged in a conversation with your teenager in which you are calm and cool.* Hear yourself saying something like, "I know football is very important to you and I am glad that you are interested in something that trains your mind and your body. At the same time, I feel that I need to help you understand that your courses come first and that it is just as important to keep up your grades by doing your homework. You have told me that you want to go to college and I want to support you with that goal. Think about it. Your grades are going to matter when you apply to college. I don't want you to be disappointed by not having the grades to get into the college you choose."

6. ***I know, I know. It all seems so easy when you are imagining it.***
   But as you work on seeing yourself calm, cool, and logical
   in your imagination, you will be helping yourself remain
   that way when you are actually dealing with your child
   about homework. You might also plan to get up half an
   hour earlier on the morning that you have to have this conversation with your teenager. Plan to have your first cup of
   coffee alone and in silence. That way you'll be relaxed and
   your nerves won't be on edge by the time your teenager
   gets up and you begin to talk about that homework.

7. ***Keep getting more and more specific with your visualizations.***
   For example, if you are always having arguments on the
   phone with your beloved but cantankerous mother when
   you are at work, picture yourself eliminating the stress of
   arguments by calling her only in the evenings. Call her
   after you have had your dinner and had a chance to relax.
   Decide not to call her during the day when you are being
   pressed by your boss to get a project out.

8. *Avoid thinking that a plan toward a goal has to be an elaborate one.* Recognize the fact that, when you are working toward an emotional or psychological goal, very often the simpler the steps the more likely they are to be successful.

9. *Understand and accept the fact that emotional and psychological goals are just as legitimate as concrete career or professional goals.*

10. *Keep reviewing and refining your plan as events evolve.* Decide to talk to a trusted friend about your situation and get his or her advice. If someone you know and trust appears to have a satisfactory relationship or what you consider a healthy home life, talk to that person and find out what they do, what tips they may have to offer. Seek out people who have points of view that you value. Include in your plan professional counseling if, in your opinion, that is what is needed for your emotional and psychological goals to come to fruition. Then add a step-by-step process for acquiring and using that professional help. Keep those appointments.

All goals are achievable

I believe that all goals as long as they are positive and uplifting in nature are achievable. But in order to attain them you have to have a plan that is *definite and specific.* It can't be hit-and-miss, on-again and off-again, or fuzzy and vague.

You have to stick with the plan for your goal to be achieved. *You* have to stick with it. No other person can do that for you.

Be a rockhead

Writing this reminds me of a nickname my grandmother used to call me. It was rockhead.

One day I asked her, "Gran, why do you call me rockhead?"

She laughed and said, "It's because, for a child, you can be so determined and stubborn sometimes. When you make up your mind about something you can stick to it no matter what happens or what anyone says about it."

As I was growing up there were many times when I didn't

know whether being a rockhead was a good thing or not. However, when I began to work on my pearls of wisdom, I recalled that rockhead nickname and I used that trait to keep me on track, working steadfastly on my plan, whatever it happened to be at the time.

And I've come to realize that that rockhead trait has really helped me weather the storms that arose and overcome the obstacles that rose up before me. I no longer feel the least bit ambivalent about it.

My advice to you is that it might be good to take on a little of that rockhead tendency as you create your plans toward your goals. Come up with your own nickname for yourself. Smile as you say it to yourself. Don't let anything or anyone discourage you from doing it.

Make your plan and work your plan

Remember, the most logical, beautiful, exciting plan in the world will not help you if it is just sitting there on paper or just

flipping around in your mind. Once you have the blueprint —
your plan — you have to get started on the path to your goal.

The ABCs — how to work it

𝓐. YOU'VE DECIDED WHAT IT IS YOU'D LIKE TO ACCOM-
PLISH TO MAKE YOUR LIFE MORE SATISFYING. This is
your goal or dream. Get started on it. Don't just sit there. What
is it going to take? Do you already have some idea about what
it will take? If you do, fine. Start to draw up a step-by-step
road map, even if you are not sure what all the steps are. And if
you're not sure, ask around. Call the library. Talk to your
friends about what it may take to get to your goal. Talk to your
boss. That's doing research. It doesn't have to be complicated,
but you have to have some knowledge about what it takes to
do what you want to do before you start toward it.

𝓑. AFTER YOU HAVE DONE YOUR RESEARCH AND GATHERED
YOUR DATA, STUDY YOUR FINDINGS. Steep yourself in the

knowledge by reviewing it in depth, turning it over in your mind. And don't say you are too busy to do this, that you'll do it when you have time. You do have time right now. Find the time by eliminating the things that take up your spare time and that are not really getting you anywhere. We all have that kind of time. This is the time we use feeling sorry for ourselves or criticizing others. This is the time we spend in front of the television. Cut down on those activities and use that time wisely. Turn your dining table into a work station for your plan so you can't avoid it.

C. DO DRAFTS, ACTUAL WRITTEN DRAFTS, OF YOUR PLAN TO YOUR GOALS AND DREAMS. Review and redo your drafts until all the elements are clear. You don't have to rush. You don't even have to tell anyone if you don't need to. Sometimes this adds to the excitement. Don't rush yourself, thrive in the process of your plan's planned execution.

The Pearl *of* ACTUATE

"Do" is the critical word.
—Peter F. Drucker

Get off the dime

*I*n the same way that you used the other pearls, begin to work your plan every day. Listen to what your heart tells you, use those gut feelings, follow those hunches.

Jo Anne Chase tells us, "Your dreams can come true...by listening, looking, learning—you can bring into your life the deepest desires of your heart."

You can't sit and wait for your dreams to come true, you must move toward your goals. This accounts for the difference between the achievers and the dreamers.

A retired man I know was bored with his life to the point where his health was being affected. He drifted into a pattern of always having a litany of aches and pains that he liked to talk about. One day a friend of his pinned him to the wall with the question of what, if anything, would make him happy. It started the man thinking about dreams he had had when he was young about traveling all over the world. He had put those aside when he went to work and started a family.

But recalling those long ago fantasies caused him to think about how he could make his old dreams come true. He was a widower and his children were all grown and on their own, so he had no responsibilities that chained him to one spot. As he continued to think about his dreams he started paying attention to his hunches.

One day he saw an ad in the newspaper placed by a cruise ship line seeking hosts for various cruises. The ad struck a chord with him. Instantly he jumped on that opportunity and applied. One of the basic requirements was the ability to dance, and this fellow really knew how to cut a rug. He also had no difficulty in meeting and talking with strangers and those were outstanding skills for a cruise ship host.

Of course he got the job. And now he is happy and fulfilled, traveling around the world. His aches and pains have subsided, all because he followed a hunch and activated the steps to his dream career.

You must actuate your dreams by tackling at least one step on your plan each and every day. Heeding your hunches and following up has to be continuous. You must make acting on your instincts and gut feelings a practice that you acquire and use.

Specifics

If your goal is a certain job, do at least one thing toward that goal every day. It could be as simple a thing as passing in front of the building where the job is located, standing in front of the building for a minute or two, and concentrating on seeing yourself going into the doorway of the building to the job.

Go ahead and laugh. I know that what I just said may sound silly and some of you may be thinking that I've really flipped on this one. But believe me, this can work.

The reason it will work is because the act of standing in front of the building is helping you to concentrate on your goal of getting the job there. It is helping you solidify your goal in your mind. That concentration allows any helpful hunches to come to the fore and allows you to act on those hunches.

What I did

One time I wanted a particular job. I used my ten pearls program and concentrated on getting the position. To help myself concentrate on that job and actuate my plan to get the job, I would pass in front of the building where the company I wanted the job with was housed. Some days I would walk past and some days I would drive past. But every day I would pass that building and spend a minute or two stopped in front of it, whether I was on foot or in my car. At times it all seemed kind of silly, but I did it anyway because it helped me keep the thought of getting that job in my mind.

One morning as I stopped in front of the building, I had a thought to find out who was on the board of directors. Most organizations, public or private, have boards that oversee the running of the institution and have a say about what goes on in the organization. Following up on that hunch I got a list of the members of the board. None of the names were familiar to me. After asking around, however, I found that I had three friends who knew two board members each. I asked them to put in a good word for me. All three friends felt that my skill level and background were appropriate for the job, and all three were familiar with what the organization needed in the position that was available. So none of them minded mentioning my application to the people they knew on that board.

It really is simple

So you see, the practice of passing in front of the building led me to a hunch, which, with follow-through on my part, helped me get known to a few of the people who would be making the decision about the hire. The operative element here is the fact that I heeded and acted on that original instinct.

Passing in front of the building also made me think about the job often and caused me to be alert to any information that I would come across about the company. I mentally stored that information in my mind and I planned to use it if I was successful in getting an interview.

In the meantime I had actuated the usual steps involved in getting the job. I sent in an application and a résumé. Eventually I was called for an interview. Acting on all the information I had learned about the organization, I had put together what I thought was an excellent presentation to the search committee. But despite all of my concentration and action, I didn't get the job.

Even if it's a bummer — stay energized

Was I disappointed? Yes. Did I feel that I had wasted my time?
Yes. Did I go on to another job? Yes. And it was a good, solid job.

However, even then, whenever I passed in front of the building that housed the original firm, I would feel kind of wistful.
I liked the job I had, but something in the back of my mind still
made me think that the first job was the one for me.

Two years later I found out that the original job was open
again. Immediately I went into action by sending the application
packet again and alerting my network of contacts about my
interest. I also restarted my practice of passing the building and
picking up and acting on any hunches that surfaced during my
concentration time.

Sure enough, I was called for another interview. I really
poured my heart and soul into my presentation this time. But I
got a call a few days later telling me that some other sterling
candidate had been selected.

My heart really sank, because I had been so sure I was activating my pearls in the right way. I was concentrating and immediately following through on all my hunches and instincts about getting that job. And I had been so convinced that it was perfect for me.

For a few days after that I let myself wallow in disappointment and doubt. Mentally, I retraced my steps and picked apart all my actions with regard to that job. I thought that my process had been flawed in some way and I was determined to find out what those flaws had been. Looking back I realize that the rehashing process was actually helpful because it kept that job on my mind even after I heard that I didn't get it. So in a sense I was still acting on the situation.

As it turned out, before the end of that week, I got a call and an offer for the job. It seemed that the board and the first sterling candidate couldn't agree on terms, so the board turned to its second choice, which was me. I couldn't accept the offer quickly enough.

Always act

You must do at least one thing each and every day. The action can be multifaceted and complicated or it can be as silly as standing in front of a building for a few minutes a day. The fact is that each time you take action toward your goal you are allowing your instincts to guide you. During the action you are concentrating your attention on your goal. That concentration can call up hunches that can be helpful to you if you act on them.

Do not let your head hit the pillow, in any given twenty-four hour period, without having taken at least one action toward the particular goal you are working on that day.

On some days actuating is going to seem like the hardest thing in the world to do. You will have days when you feel depressed and discouraged. You will have days when you are plagued with doubt. How do you think I felt on the day I got the call that I didn't get that job for the second time? But those will be the days and times that you have to work even harder than usual to get yourself to set in motion one act toward your goal.

You will have feelings that the whole thing is crazy, some pie in the sky, and you will want to quit. What I do at those times is to tell myself that I can quit. These are the goals that I made. Many times, no one else even knows about them, so there is no one in a position to flog me on. But sometimes the very fact of knowing that I can quit working on a particular goal if I want to actually helps me stay on track and I renew my resolve by actuating some step. Also the prospect of having no goal at all in front of me is worse than the effort required to put my shoulder to the wheel again.

Your lovely dreams will just lie there in your mind or on paper if you don't take action to move down the road toward them. Louise L. Hay makes this point perfectly. She says, "If you want to move to another room, you have to get up and move step by step in that direction. Just sitting in your chair and demanding that you be in the other room will not work."

Nothing ventured, nothing gained.

The ABCs — how to work it

𝒜. YOU'VE GOT TO INVEST YOUR GOALS AND DREAMS WITH ENERGY SO THAT THEY CAN MOVE. They need to be dynamic, like the molecules that make up everything that exists. Molecules are not just sitting or standing around. They are shaking and finger-popping, as it were. They are constantly on the go. The actions you take toward your goals have to be constant — hyperactive in a sense.

ℬ. FLASHES, HUNCHES, GUT FEELINGS ARE FLEETING. They don't stay around long. They flit across your mind and then they are gone, like a falling comet. You have to be alert so that you can grab hold and then understand these insights. You have to be a quick study, get the understanding, and then mobilize. Do the first thing that comes to your mind in the morning about your goal. If you linger, you give time for all the doubt and uncertainty that is waiting in the wings to zap you, to dissipate your understanding. And you don't want that to happen.

C. WHEN YOU GET YOUR FLASHES OR HUNCHES OF THE DAY, MOVE ON THEM *THAT* DAY. Some of them will pan out for you and others might be dead ends. Still, the time you have spent is not wasted because you are programming yourself to be alert. This alert state will cause you to pick up on the next insight sooner and with more understanding. The actuating process will also generate excitement within you about your goals and dreams. This results in a kind of self-charging process that makes your resolve stronger. You are building momentum that propels you forward. *Act now!*

The Pearl *of* HABITUATE

When you have know-how, *you can do that something successfully again and again. It's a habit, and it comes naturally from experience.*
—W. Clement Stone

Over and over and over again

One of my favorite musicals is *My Fair Lady,* and I always enjoy the scene where Professor Higgins is telling Eliza Doolittle to repeat the phrase she's working on. He just keeps saying "again." It reminds me of using the pearl of habituate. The point of this pearl is to constantly, on a daily basis, work on your pearls until using them becomes a habit. Habits are hard to break and positive habits are just as hard to break as negative ones. You need to make using your pearls of wisdom toward your goals such a part of your daily life that it becomes habitual.

We all have habits, inclinations to do things in a certain way, inclinations that have become second nature to us. This is exactly what you want to achieve with your pearls of wisdom. They have to become automatic.

In the early days of growing my pearls I thought making them a habit was the hardest step of all, but I've changed my mind. Positive habits all depend on the payoff or benefits that one derives from them. For me the payoff for using the pearls of wisdom is the ability to achieve each and every goal I set.

Concentration is magnetic

The best way to make using the pearls habitual is to start getting some goals under your belt. Begin with small goals that may not seem very important and work on them one at a time. Remember the goal I had of finding just the right dress at just the right price? And remember how achieving that goal spurred me to believe in my pearls and work on bigger goals?

Begin with goals like that one. As those little goals start mounting up, your own exhilaration will spark you to continue to believe in and use your pearls.

Concentration on your goals and dreams and following up on your hunches is crucial. Making that process a habit means always being aware of your flashes of thought related to your goals and always acting on those flashes.

Say you want a job at a certain company and you add getting that job to your goal list. During your daily concentration time you remember that you met someone who worked at the company some time back and you think that that person may have given you her card. You catch the flash and dig the card out. You call her and express interest in a job at the company. By paying attention and acting on your hunch you have brought yourself that much closer to your goal.

It could turn out that there are no job openings at the moment. But even if that's the case you can still use the opportunity to quiz your contact and get more information either about that company or other companies you may be interested in joining. The point is that by getting in the habit of catching your flashes and following your hunches you start on a path

that is leading you closer and closer to your goal. All of your contacts might not result immediately in achievement of your goal, but often you can gain something that will take you closer.

Payoff can come years later

I credit the habit of paying attention to my hunches as the reason I got the job I have now. I had met the headhunters who referred me to this job some years ago when they recruited a staffer who came to work for me at another agency. During that process one of them asked me to lunch to discuss the possibility of helping us fill other positions that were open. On the day of the lunch appointment I had two or three unplanned events occur at work and I almost canceled. But as I had picked up the phone to call and cancel I had a flash that said don't do it.

And so, because I have made a habit of listening to and acting on my hunches, I put the phone down and met with the headhunter. That firm did end up doing some recruiting for our agency. But years passed after that and I didn't hear anything more from them.

Then, lo and behold, I got a call out of the blue from the headhunter I had had lunch with that day telling me about the fabulous job I have now. If I had not followed my habit of obeying my hunches and kept that original appointment, I might not have been on the list of those he contacted about the job.

Train yourself

One of my friends sustains her habit of using her pearls by setting her watch to sound an alarm every two hours. When it buzzes, she stops and records any thought she has about her goals on a little notepad she carries with her. Then at the end of her work day she reads her notes and follows up on any hunches that appeal to her at that particular time. She has fun picking the one she works on that day.

One of her hobbies is writing poetry. She tells a lovely

story about how she followed a hunch to stop and buy her-self a beautiful bouquet of flowers one day. As she sat that evening enjoying the fragrance of the flowers, she was inspired to write what she considers her best poem yet.

Help yourself grow the habit

In order to help yourself develop the habit of using your pearls of wisdom, concentrating on your goals, and acting on your hunches and instincts about your goals you might want to try one of the tools I have used over the years. I list my current goals in my little journal and when I have a few free minutes during the day, I take it out and read them. I do this when I'm under the hair dryer, or waiting for my son to come out of basketball practice, or waiting for someone I'm meeting for lunch. I've learned to fill those time gaps that would just be wasted with an activity that is positive for me, habitualizing my use of the pearls of wisdom and concentrating on my goals.

One of my friends keeps a piece of cardboard with his

goals written on it in the glove compartment of his car. When
he reaches in to get his garage door opener, he's reminded of
his ten pearls and checks his hunches. Another man I know
has written his goals on a luggage tag that he has attached to
his key chain. Whenever he uses his keys he gets a chance to
think about his goals. One guy keeps a note pad in his jacket
pocket and pulls it out from time to time to look at his list of
goals as he goes through his day. He jots down any hunches
he has in a kind of shorthand that he has made up.

Granny's view

"Practice makes perfect" was one of my grandmother's
favorite expressions. She encouraged us to do things over
and over until we got into the habit of doing them well.
When I was learning to sew, if my seams were not straight,
she would insist that I take out the stitches and sew the
seam again. Although I would get impatient with her for
doing things like that, I look back now and realize that what

she was doing was encouraging me to form positive habits. She wanted me to do things over and over again, until doing them right became second nature to me.

I'm grateful to her. And I'm urging you to keep concentrating and following your hunches over and over again until it becomes a practice that is perfect for you.

Working my pearls of wisdom is so habitual for me now that I find that I am not able to go to sleep until I have done a review of the pearls and the particular goals I am working on at that time. I can't even doze before I do it.

That's because I have mastered the pearl of habituate. And, I assure you, that when you have mastered this pearl, it will work the same way for you.

The ABCs — how to work it

A. ESTABLISHING THE HABIT OF BEING ALERT TO YOUR INSTINCTS AND USING YOUR PEARLS OF WISDOM IS JUST AS EASY AS ESTABLISHING THE HABIT OF PUTTING THE CAP

ON THE TOOTHPASTE OR DROPPING YOUR DIRTY CLOTHES
IN THE HAMPER RATHER THAN ON THE BEDROOM FLOOR.
It becomes something you do because, it seems, you have
always done it. And it is just as easy to cultivate good
habits as bad ones. With bad ones, however, the outcome
is usually an irate mate or guilt. So concentrate on those
habits that strengthen your sense of order and progress.

B. I WANT TO REPEAT THAT THIS IS YOUR LIFE. You can
use your time in activities that are fulfilling and positive
for you or not. It's all your choice. I'm urging you to
make the choice of using your time and brain power to
help you achieve your goals and dreams.

C. IN YOUR FREE HOURS, OR EVEN YOUR FREE MINUTES DUR-
ING THE DAY, GROW YOUR HABIT OF FOCUSING ON YOUR
GOALS AND DREAMS.

The Pearl *of* PRETEND

There is no greater force at your service than your own mind
coupled with a strong, positive self image.
—Dennis Kimbro, Ph.D.

It can be fun

You are preparing for an important meeting and you can feel yourself tensing up to the point where your head aches. You would love to interact in the meeting calmly, coolly, and capably but you just know you are going to blow it. Stop. Calm down. Sit back and take a deep breath. Take another. Now pretend that you are sitting in the meeting with a smile on your face and your flawless reports in your hand. Keep that picture in your mind. Think about it over and over again. Hear yourself speaking in your mind. After five minutes, get up and go to the meeting. As you walk along the hallway, keep focusing on your mental picture of yourself calm as a cucumber. Lay that cucumber in the middle of the conference room table and keep your mental eye on it. I guarantee it will help you.

Fantasy can become reality

I pretend all the time. I call this the fun pearl because I enjoy it so much. When I set a goal I always spend some time within my fifteen minutes of concentration mentally picturing myself as I will be after I have achieved the goal. I focus on seeing in my mind and feeling in my heart whatever will be different once I have attained the goal. I am, in essence, living the goal before it actually materializes. I am also positioning myself to be receptive to any hunches or gut instincts about the goal that can help me attain it. I become in tune with anything and everything that can assist me with getting there.

One time I set a goal of achieving excellent posture. And during my daily fifteen minutes of concentration I decided to pretend that I was a queen. I have never seen or heard of any queen who didn't stand, walk, or sit straight. In my mind I

began to picture myself as a queen and saw myself walking in ceremonial processions, standing at attention receiving my court, and sitting on my throne. When this picture would flash into my mind, I would remind myself to throw back my shoulders and hold my head high. After about three months of this pretending, I noticed that my posture had improved tenfold.

You're using the time anyway

Let's say that you are preparing for a date with someone you have fantasized about for months. It's finally happening. But you are nervous. You can't make up your mind about what to wear. You are convinced you will make some gaffe and never see the wonderful one again. All of these horrible pictures that you are allowing to march through your mind are pretend situations. The scenes you focus on are not really happening. You are imagining them. And you've worked yourself up into an agitated state about nothing. Really. Haven't you? You've used time and nervous energy thinking about disaster. You're pretending all that time.

Turn that around. Use the time that you would be using anyway, in a manner that can help you with your goal of impressing your date. Make yourself form a picture, a pretend situation, differently. Start to see yourself in your best, most flattering outfit and feeling that you look irresistible to your dream date. Imagine the two of you in the restaurant talking and laughing together and having a great time. If you want to be perceived as witty and charming, see yourself as witty and charming. Imagine your bons mots. Mentally hear yourself rolling them off your tongue with panache. Pretend that your dinner partner is mesmerized by your charm. Hear that person telling you just that. It takes no more time and effort to pretend this sort of picture than it takes to imagine yourself spilling your wine and dying of embarrassment.

Who says it's not real

Remember, in the introduction of this book, when I told about my friend who had the goal of going to Paris? She pretended all the time. In her mind she saw herself landing at Charles De Gaulle Airport and being whisked away to a lovely apartment. She imagined herself getting up in the morning and throwing open the windows to hear the Paris church bells. Her pretending kept the trip on her mind and poised her to catch each and every instinct that came to her about her goal. And, of course, she acted on every hunch. Eventually her dream became real. Voilà!

And you can help yourself while enjoying it

What you are doing when you pretend is honing a self-image that is in harmony with your goal. And self-image is a powerful tool. In his book *Think and Grow Rich: A Black Choice*, Dennis Kimbro expressed this tenet. He wrote, "The self-image is a premise, a base or foundation upon which your entire personality and behavior is built. Because of this, your experiences seem to verify, and thereby strengthen, your self-image, creating a positive or negative impact." The title of

Dr. Wayne W. Dyer's book *You Will See It When You Believe It*
expresses the same point.

Pretending also gives you a chance to act out everything and
to pick and choose your own actions and reactions. Playacting
beforehand helps you recall those choices when you are actually
faced with the goal you've prepared yourself for. The activity of
picking and choosing your actions and reactions allows you to
catch flashes of information that can be signposts for you.

Serious business

After I had heard from the headhunter and had decided to set
the goal of obtaining the job I have now, I immediately began
to pretend that I was already experiencing the stages that
would lead to the job. During my concentration I would
pretend that I was sitting in the interview with the search committee. And I pretended that I was answering their questions.

To prepare myself for the questions, I pretended that I
was one of the members. I asked myself, if that were so, what

my questions would be. This thought led me to decide to research everything I could find out about the agency so that I could study that material and be prepared to answer any question. I requested and received the agency brochures. I called colleagues in the field who worked in the area where the agency was located and asked them questions. I went to the library and checked newspaper articles that had mentioned the organization.

By pretending I was a board member I was able to formulate questions that I thought would be important to ask a candidate. I mentally placed myself in a board member's shoes and role-played questions that I felt would be pertinent. Then, again pretending, I saw myself in the candidate's chair, the hot seat as it were; and I mentally answered each and every question. During this pretending process, I'd flash on questions that I had not thought of before. I followed up on those flashes by delving into the material I had collected about the agency and boning up on those points. All of this pretending and following through on my hunches about the situation made me rock solid ready when it came time to attend the interview, and filled me with the confidence that comes from thorough preparation.

It's not complicated

Pretending that you have already reached your goal is simple and easy. It's just playacting, imagining something that doesn't exist. We do it all the time. And no one can ridicule you about it because you can choose not to tell anyone that you are doing it. Over the years, however, I have found it pleasant to share my goals with people who are close to me; and sometimes they can help me with my pretending. I shared my method of achieving good posture with friends and their teasing kept me on track. I'd be walking down the hallway at work, for example, and if I was slouching someone would call out "Watch it, madam queen." We would laugh together, but at the same time it was a reminder that helped me.

Help with harmony

One time I worked with a woman who in addition to her full-time job had a husband and three teenage children. She was always complaining about how hectic her home life was and how that made her miserable. "Bicker, bicker, bicker is all we seem to do," she reported. In a discussion the two of us were having about the ten pearls, she really perked up at the pearl of pretend and she made up her mind to focus on that pearl. She was skeptical at first but she said that it sounded easy and she was going to try it.

She began to take a fifteen minute break at the end of the work day, before she would leave the office. She'd sit in her chair and imagine herself going through the activities of the evening—driving, arriving home, greeting her family, starting dinner, eating it, then washing up, relaxing with a book, watching television, or having a conversation with her husband while the kids did homework. In her mind she pretended that everything was smooth and tension free. Then she'd leave for home.

"It's not working," she told me about three weeks after she tried pretending for the first time. "I stop and sit and imagine how the evening is going to be and nothing works out the way I see it in my mind." I asked her to give me more details. "Take last night," she said, "I had pictured sitting and enjoying a bouquet of flowers from Joe. I also pictured Helen telling me that she had washed and ironed the skirt that she needed for the dance instead of asking me to do it. She hadn't. It was still in the laundry hamper. I had pretended that Lilly had already started dinner. Instead I found the stove cold as ice and my oldest daughter curled up on the couch with a magazine. Nothing was the way I saw it in my mind."

I commiserated with her discouragement for a few minutes. And then I suggested that she start all over again. This time, during her fifteen-minute break, she was to imagine her pictures, but she was only to concentrate on what she herself

was doing. I emphasized that the only thing we can really predict or control, in any given event, are our own actions and reactions. We can wish, hope, and hint about the actions of others but we can never guarantee those actions.

I suggested that instead of seeing her husband bringing her a bouquet of flowers, she should stop off and buy them for herself before she got home. By doing this she could be sure that the flowers she pictured herself enjoying would definitely be there that night.

I also suggested that before she left for work in the morning, she actually tell her children what specific chores she wanted them to do by the time she got home, rather than just willing them to know what they should do. And that she should let them know that if they didn't do the chores, she wasn't going to do them, so they would have to live with that fact. Above all, I encouraged her to concentrate on a picture of herself acting and reacting to whatever she might find when she got home and to remove any actions or reactions that she did not like or want to have.

She started her pretend sessions again and eventually reported that she was learning to control herself by concentrating on how she wanted to interact with her family. By seeing herself in her mental pictures as calm and cool, she found herself feeling less tense by the time she got to her door. And because of this mental picture she was able to keep herself from getting upset no matter what hell was breaking loose on the home front.

A little humming can go a long way

"I just go into my dream world," she said. "In my pretend sessions I see myself arriving home and floating through what I have to do with a smile on my face. During one visualization I imagined that I could hear myself humming. And I remembered that I used to hum tunes all the time and that it used to calm me down when I was upset. I had stopped doing that years ago. But when it popped into my mental picture, I took up the practice again."

It took many months of pretending on her part, and there were many times when she would get discouraged. But after a while, the fact that she could keep calm began to influence her family members. "At first they just stared at me like they thought I was crazy when I would smile and hum my way through some domestic flap," she said, "but then they started calming down too."

Keep it light but take it seriously

Start using pretend with small goals, things that won't devastate you if you don't achieve them right away. But make yourself focus on mental pictures of the end result. Playact how you will look, feel, and be after you have gotten where you want to go. While concentrating on that picture take note of any hunches that may come to you and act on them. They may seem unimportant, but they can help. My friend's practice of humming seemed inconsequential, but it was a major tool for her to use to keep herself calm.

Once you become grounded in the practice of pretending, you can use it on all your goals, big and small, objective and emotional. When you set a goal immediately begin to see yourself in your mind as already having achieved it. Pretend — and become what you dream of becoming.

The ABCs — how to work it

A. IN A LOT OF WAYS, PRETEND IS THE EASIEST PEARL OF ALL. It won't work just by itself, but it can certainly be a sweetener and a respite in your daily process of activity toward your goal achievement. It's totally private so you are not subjecting yourself to any kind of ridicule when you use it. More important, it's drawing your goals to you and kind of pulling and pushing you at the same time.

B. THE SERIOUS PART OF PRETEND IS USING THE ACTIVITY OF SEEING YOURSELF AS YOU WILL BE WHEN YOU REACH YOUR GOAL AND TO HELP YOU POLISH THAT IMAGE.

And as you grow more astute with using pretend, you will come to the place where you can pick out any flaws in the image of your glorious future in time to remove them before you get there.

C. ONE OF THE MOST IMPORTANT THINGS ABOUT PRETEND IS THE FACT THAT THE CONCENTRATION INVOLVED IS SERVING AS A MAGNET FOR YOUR DREAMS AND GOALS. Remember my grandmother's favorite saying, "What you follow, follows you." You get what you concentrate on, you become what you see yourself becoming in your mind. Very few successful people report that they are totally surprised when they have attained their particular accomplishments. Most of them report that they somehow knew that they would get what they worked toward. I think that, in one way or another, they have used the pearl of pretend.

The Pearl *of* REFINE

With every disadvantage, there is always a greater advantage.
—W. Clement Stone

Enhancing your pearl

The more beautiful the pearl, the more smoothly each layer of nacre has flowed over the previous one. By the time the pearl is removed from the oyster shell, it is perfect. It has no bumps, nicks, or cracks.

When you use the pearl of refine, you focus on the picture of yourself as you will be when you have reached your goal; and you work with that picture so that any imperfections or enhancements needed to make the picture perfect are revealed. Then you smooth out these imperfections or add those enhancements as you use your ten pearls on a daily basis. You do this so that by the time you reach your goal, you are ready for it in every way. And — as your mental image changes and grows — the daily activities toward your goals change as well.

To illustrate what I mean, I'd like to go back to the early goal I set to return to college and get my degree.

1. *After I began to visualize myself at the graduation ceremony that was to take place three years into the future, I started to take a hard look at that image and search my mind to identify what would need to happen for that picture to become a reality.*

2. *I knew I didn't have the money to pay the tuition so I accepted the fact that I would have to get a scholarship or a grant.* The grades I had earned toward my degree in the night school courses I had taken previously were not high enough for a scholarship. So, early on, I knew I would have to go for a grant. I started researching and applying for grants.

3. ***After I got the grant applications, I took another look at that mental picture of graduation and realized that even if I got a grant, it would only cover my school costs and I'd need money for living expenses.*** At the same time I was determined to go to school in the daytime. I had had it with night school. Working with this realization (or bump in my layer of nacre, if you will) caused me to change my work hours so that I could work in the evening and go to school during the day.

4. ***At the end of my second year of college I delved deeper into exactly what kind of position in social work I wanted after graduation.*** I had looked forward to doing counseling and therapy and I learned that I'd have to have a master's degree in order to qualify for that kind of position. This caused me to modify the mental image of myself in a cap and gown at graduation, to one of myself sitting in an office counseling individuals and couples. This refinement of my

initial mental picture made me begin applying to graduate school in the first half of my last year of college.

5. ***Mentally seeing myself sitting in an office doing therapy caused me to start to research job possibilities and send out my résumé before I actually finished my studies.*** Those activities led me to having three job offers on the day I received my master's degree. I chose one of those jobs and went to work.

Starting with my mental image of myself at my goal of graduation from college, I had continued to visualize and grow that image and act on that image every time I mentally discerned a bump, or nick in my perfect picture. The bumps included not having tuition, having to change my work hours, and having to have a master's degree to do the kind of social work I had dreamed of doing. I was refining every step of the way. And by the time I reached my goal, I was on solid ground and ready to succeed in the profession I had chosen.

The refinements of others

Remember my friend who went to Paris? She did a lot of refining as she visualized her dream. As she mentally saw herself in Paris, she realized that she wanted to be dressed nicely. Again, money was a factor. But before she even knew exactly where she was going to stay when she got there, she started seeing herself, in her mental image, as having a wonderful outfit to wear on every day of her visit.

Refining this image, she began to see herself in colorful costumes. She's a tall, strikingly beautiful woman and she looks stunning in dramatic outfits. To prepare to knock Paris off its feet with her looks, she started combing the secondhand clothing shops on a weekly basis. She found scarves, blouses, skirts, and accessories, for very little money and put them together. In her journal she began to describe the specific outfits that she would wear to certain places in Paris. "This is what I'm going to wear when I visit art museums," she would

say as she modeled some of her outfits for us. "I'm wearing this out to dinner," she added as she modeled a lovely turban she had made from two of her scarves. Daily use of her mental pictures caused her to constantly refine the image. Acting on her refinement process, she made certain that she would be dressed to thrill.

Style as smooth as silk

I know another woman who wanted to be a cabaret singer and she began to use that mental image to guide herself as she worked toward that goal. Each time she visualized herself singing on a stage, she would concentrate on that mental picture and dissect what she saw.

She decided that she needed to lose weight in order to be as attractive as she could be. She dieted and lost twenty pounds. Then she decided that she wanted to have a signature look and she made herself five outfits, all in black.

Then she began to enlarge her mental image so it included

the audience she would be singing to. She wanted the audience to feel the words of her songs and to respond to them; she knew that she would have to work on her innate shyness and let her own feelings flow while she sang. Looking back, she says that in her initial image she saw herself as standing stiffly and "singing with perfection, but no heart."

Her favorite songs were ballads and love songs filled with romance and longing. She wanted to convey these emotions and touch her listeners. She started picturing individual people in her imaginary audience. People who had fallen in love and lost. People who had fallen in love and lived happily. She began to use the emotions that she felt when she sang to loosen up her delivery and she pictured people who had had the same experiences listening to her sing and recalling their own love stories. Slowly she began to smooth out each imperfection that she perceived in her mental images.

Through using the pearl of refine, she went on to perfect her act to the point where her performance was described by

one nightclub music critic as being "reminiscent of Nancy Wilson"—who happened to be one of her singing idols. She cut that review out of the newspaper, had it framed, and hung it on her wall. Looking at it reminds her to continue refining and perfecting her performances.

The best it can be

Using the pearl of refine means seeing the image of yourself and how you will be when you achieve your goal and polishing that image until it is perfect. In this way you are ready to accept success and all of its facets. You have polished it, you have honed it, and now you can enjoy the achievement in comfort.

The ABCs—how to work it

A. YOU'VE HEARD OF PEOPLE WHO RETIRE FROM A JOB OR CAREER THEY HAVE HAD FOR A LONG TIME, AND THEN FIND THEMSELVES AT A LOSS AS TO WHAT TO DO WITH THEIR TIME. My theory is that they probably dreamed about retiring and even worked very hard to accumulate the financial resources that would be available when the income from the job stopped. They probably even pretended or visualized themselves waking up every morning and turning over to go back to sleep instead of getting dressed and leaving the house to go to work. But they did not visualize what they would be doing once they retired. Refine makes you ready. If your dream is retiring I think that you should certainly concentrate on it. But I also think that as you wait for that dream to be realized, you should also study what you are going to do with all that free time. Find yourself a favorite charity where you can volunteer. Get that catalog from the local junior college and find out about courses in that other language that you've always wanted to be able to speak. Do you like baseball? Why not plan to coach a little league team? That's using the pearl of refine.

ℬ. YOU'RE GOING TO ACHIEVE YOUR DREAMS. If you believe this, then you owe it to yourself to be as ready for them as you can be.

ℭ. REFINE MAKES YOU READY. Using this pearl assures that when you, the great French chef, open that restaurant of your dreams, you've done your research and know that there are not four other French restaurants within a two-mile radius of your place. Refine makes you ready. Using it assures you that when you finally court and marry the person who is the love of your life, you will be ready to share that life. If that person happens to thrive on symphony music and has had season tickets for the past ten years, you have boned up on Beethoven and know that there will be no trouble in paradise over your lack of appreciation for fine music. Refine means becoming aware of, understanding, and smoothing out those little imperfections in your dream before they come true.

The Pearl *of* CLAIM

If something is for you, you can get it.
—Eleanor Brooks Johnson

You deserve it

Claim is a very serious pearl of wisdom. And it can be the hardest to implement. The premise of the pearl is this: *It is necessary for you to feel that you deserve your goals and dreams in order for you to achieve them and keep them.*

After many years of working in the field of social work, a field heavily influenced by the accepted theories of human behavior, I have come to the conclusion that a lot of the failure and unhappiness we see around us is due to the fact that many individuals do not feel that they are worthy of achievement and success. These individuals do not have a strong sense of self-worth.

We hear a lot about self-esteem. I have tried to define, for myself, what I mean by that phrase when I use it. To me, to have a sense of self-worth means to believe that you as an individual are deserving of whatever you consider positive or best for you. It means that you have the ability, within yourself, to convince yourself that you have a right to acquire or claim whatever you choose as good for you. This is what my grandmother meant when she would say, "If something is for you, you can get it." She meant that if whatever you have chosen is good and right for you, you can get it, it will come to you. This may not be what someone else considers good for you, but it must be what you consider good for yourself.

At the same time I am stating that *only you can decide what is best for you.* You cannot abdicate this decision to someone else in your life and expect that things will turn out all right. You must take ownership of your own destiny. You must be prepared to decide for yourself, examine all of your decisions carefully, and then proceed with what is best for you in view of the values you accept.

It has to be yours

For a program like the ten pearls of wisdom to work, the person using the program has to have a solid sense that they deserve what it is they desire. That may sound silly.

"Of course," you may say in a glib manner, "I think that I deserve the best."

We hear this often. Yet, how many times is that actually true? How many of us really, consistently, feel that we deserve the best? In *Think and Grow Rich: A Black Choice*, Dennis Kimbro tells us:

> *Think for a moment of those whom you pass on the street, no matter how large or small the city, no matter its location, and regardless of the race or creed of its inhabitants—only five out of one hundred people will achieve their financial goals.* Only 5 percent! *And what of the other 95 percent? Unfortunately, they will just drift along, hoping and wishing that something positive will "turn up" or at least that nothing negative will. These are able-bodied*

men and women who've allowed the winds of circumstances to blow them in any direction.

Startling idea isn't it? And, at the same time, I'll bet that if someone polled these same people as to whether or not they think they deserve the best, most of them would answer in the affirmative. But do they really think that deep down? Do they feel, consistently, over time that they deserve the best? I think that there are many more people who just say that they deserve the best—than there are people who are genuinely convinced that they deserve the best.

Unless you are genuinely convinced that you deserve the best, you will not succeed. If, somehow, you do manage to reach your goals, you will not keep them.

There is an old saying that states that when you are ready for something (an occurrence or event or some gain that you might be seeking), it will present itself. Additionally, if you are not ready for whatever your goal or dream is, it will not present itself.

Claiming the new you

As you work with your ten pearls of wisdom and start achieving some of your goals and dreams, you will find that you are no longer the same person you were when you started. You will begin to look and feel different to yourself. You will describe yourself differently.

Gradually you will begin to look and act differently to those around you, your family and friends. You will have changed.

This is the point where the pearl of claim must be understood. When this inevitable change happens, when you begin achieving goals, there may be a negative reaction. It can come from you and it can come from those closest to you. This is because change, any kind of change, is difficult to accept.

You will begin to think, "Wait a minute, this is different. This feels funny." Those impressions can be so strong that you find yourself running back to the comfort of your former state.

It's like wearing a pair of new shoes. Their initial discomfort might send you back to the closet to get out your old pair. They are more comfortable. You neglect the new pair, even though they are sitting there shiny and beautiful. It becomes too much trouble to bear the discomfort that occurs until the new pair of shoes is broken in.

That can happen with goals. The new heights or the new situations that occur after you have achieved the goal or dream can feel like the new pair of shoes.

Many times you may find that your mate, or relatives, or friends will begin to discourage the new you. They may begin to accuse you of trying to be more than you are or trying to deny who you really are. They may begin to call you "high and mighty." And that can hurt you to the point where you abandon your goal, or your growth toward your goal, so that you won't be an outcast. You don't want to be lonely or alienated and you don't want to feel guilty about having achieved something that sets you apart.

Stay your course

Instead of giving in to those feelings of loneliness and guilt, you must train yourself to feel that any success you achieve is your due. And you must use your strand of pearls of wisdom to help you in this process. You need to also realize that you may, ultimately, have to gravitate to new relationships. Sometimes it happens that family members, friends, and others with whom you were close are uncomfortable with the ways in which you have been changed by your success.

I am not, in any way, suggesting that it is absolutely necessary for successful achievers to abandon their roots in order to live with and sustain their success. What I am saying, however, is that that does happen in some cases and that it may turn out to be the case with you. You need to know and understand that such occurrences could be a result of your having achieved your goals and captured your dreams. And you have to decide for yourself what to do about it.

If you know in your heart that the goals and dreams you are working on are right for you, then you must go with them. And, sometimes, the opinions of others in your life may be in conflict with what you think. You must convince yourself that you deserve the successes that you are working toward and, as long as you are not abusing others, you must claim them for yourself.

Listen to your heart, heed your hunches, catch and examine your flashes. If all of these instincts tell you that you are on the right road, then you can be assured that you are ready, that you deserve what you are seeking.

It's constant

Work on yourself and use your insights to grow into a state of readiness. That state of readiness will come in handy if you find that you have to fortify yourself against discouragement.

The ABCs—how to work it

A. THE PEARL OF CLAIM IS INTENSELY PERSONAL. You work on it in the depths of your mind and the core of your heart. It's easy to fool the world by expounding on your list of wonderful goals and dreams. But you can't fool yourself—at least not forever. You've got to convince yourself that you are ready for what you are seeking before you get it. Many times that conviction takes time to grow before you use it to launch yourself toward your goals and dreams. And, many times, when you listen to your heart you realize that you have some work to do with yourself before you are ready. If you feel intimidated in any way about your goals and dreams, that could be a sign that you are not totally ready for them.

B. IF THAT HAPPENS, STEP BACK. Stop yourself and work on the root of any feelings of discomfort that occur when

you visualize yourself at the heights of whatever it is you
set out to do. This can be painful for you. But you must do
it. If you see yourself as an executive of your company but
you aren't really comfortable with the mission of the enter-
prise, then you can be sure that you won't succeed even if
you get the job. If you see yourself as a congressperson,
wheeling and dealing on Capitol Hill, but you cringe every
time you have to enter a room full of strangers and shake
hands all around, you really need to explore that hesitation
in depth and resolve it before you declare your candidacy.

C. MOST OF THE WORK YOU WILL DO WITH THE PEARL
OF CLAIM IS ON THE PSYCHOLOGICAL LEVEL. It will be
an activity in your own mind, and involve your own personal emotions. And you have to learn to be very, very
honest with yourself. If you've used all the other pearls
and feel that you are ready to claim your dreams, go forward. But if you have any little flashes that something isn't

right, keep going back and starting all over again until your personal comfort level with your desires is rock solid. When you have convinced yourself that you deserve what you are seeking, you can stand firm and achieve the best of everything in your own life.

The Pearl *of* EXPAND

I go from success to success and from glory to glory.
My pathway is a series of stepping stones to ever greater successes.
—Louise L. Hay

Let your dreams soar

You are now ready for the pearl of expand, which means to widen your vision and horizons. By now, if you have been implementing the ten pearls, you are a person who has been successful at achieving some goals. You are ready to heed the urge to grow, which becomes an inevitable part of the experience of success. It will feel like you can't hold yourself back even if you try. If you have faithfully used the pearls of wisdom you will find that your mind automatically continues to move forward toward more goals.

From my personal experience I can say that unless you stopped using the pearls you could not keep yourself from expanding your limits. When you become successful, you find yourself being drawn to even more successes. It's another manifestation of that old saying, "them that has gets."

Opportunities that you could not even have imagined before you started using your pearls will begin to open up for you. People begin to give you tips and pointers when they view you as a successful person, tips that they would not even consider passing on to you if they do not see you in that light. When you achieve your goals it becomes a natural process to keep growing.

Success as a magnet

The process of growth has worked for me in all phases of my life. On my career path the growth took on a life of its own in a way. My first job out of graduate school was in direct service. Then, after a few years, I decided that I wanted to be a supervisor and I set that goal and achieved it. Working as a supervisor led me to become interested in how the policies that were used in our work, came into being. That interest caused me to seek an executive staff position so that I could work with the board of directors.

From that exposure, I gained experience and got the idea that I could be an executive director. And after working in three executive director posts, I am now the president and chief executive officer of a major human services agency. It took years and a lot of hard work, but, looking back, it all seems an inevitable outcome of the achievement of my first goal. That success became the pivot of all the activity on my career path.

The expansions of others

Remember my friend who went to Paris? She loved it so much that she made arrangements that allowed her to be able to go back for one month at least once a year. And now she's in the process of writing a travel book on Paris.

The artist who won the prestigious award has also expanded her horizons. She has become nationally known as she has traveled around the country showing her art and giving lectures. And she has also accepted a post as the head of the art department of a major university.

My friend who used the collage to remember her past successes is now running her own consulting business and doing very well. She decided she wanted to be her own boss and expanded her goal list accordingly.

The woman who started selling arts and crafts for extra income now has a sizable bank account. She has decided that she is going to establish a serious investment portfolio that will allow her to retire early, be financially independent, and not have to rely on help from her children in her senior years.

My relative who became a nurse and then moved across the country with her young son has expanded her dreams. She has gotten married and is now the mother of a beautiful little girl. She added the dream of a joyful marriage to her list and persisted until she found the right soul mate.

My retired friend is having the time of his life sailing the seven seas with the cruise line. He has also started a new career as a stand-up comic, and the cruise ship gives him the perfect outlet for his act. He's still dancing and has no aches and pains to speak of.

The poet is now exploring publication for a book of verses she has compiled from her own work and those of other poets in her circle. This is certainly a new ambition for her. She used to insist that she only wrote her poems for herself and a few friends.

The woman with the rambunctious teenagers and chaotic household has expanded her goal. Now she heads a support group for families at her church. She also reports that her home gets so quiet at times that she finds herself eagerly awaiting visits from her children and grandchildren so the house can feel full of life.

All of these are examples of individuals who set original goals, achieved them, and then went on to grow other dreams. Each success they garnered strengthened their self-confidence and made them ready to expand.

Go with the flow

Sometimes thinking about expanding can be a little scary. It goes back to those thoughts of "Can little ole me really be the boss?" But when you feel that way, start working with your strand of pearls from the beginning and take yourself, step by step, through each pearl. When I feel hesitant to expand, I immediately start using the pearl remember and I focus on mental pictures of my past successes. It's like a tonic for me. At these times, I'm also inspired by something Ralph Waldo Trine wrote in his book *In Tune with the Infinite:*

Thoughts of strength both build strength from within and attract it from without. Courage begets strength, fear begets weakness. It is the man and woman of faith, and hence of courage, who is the master of circumstances and who makes his or her own power felt in the world.

Having faith and expanding your accomplishments will become a natural and inevitable occurrence as you use the ten pearls to become successful in your life. When you feel the desire to expand, trust it and allow it to flower.

The ABCs — how to work it

A. IN SOME WAYS YOU WILL NOT HAVE TO STRAIN TO WORK ON THE PEARL OF EXPAND. It will work on you. The old saying that everyone wants to be a part of a winner is very true. As you grow and evolve as an achiever, opportunities will present themselves to you. You will inspire others around you and they will help you. You will find yourself adding the goal of helping others to the activities that you work on. I found myself doing that when I was inspired to write this book. You won't be able to stop yourself from feeling expansive — not intrusive, but expansive.

B. GROW A COMFORT LEVEL WITH THIS PEARL. See it as a natural part of your own evolution and heed your insights about new directions and challenges to undertake. See these efforts as a way to expose your strand of pearls to the world. Having a strand of pearls is certainly cause for celebration. But isn't it even more delightful when others see and enjoy it also?

C. USING THE PEARL OF EXPAND MEANS NOT HOARDING OR CLAMPING DOWN ON YOUR GOALS AND DREAMS. It means not telling yourself that once you get this goal, that's it. You have no idea what additional layers are just lying dormant waiting to flow over your grain of sand, unless you mentally open yourself to those possibilities. Never limit your dreams. Let them soar!

USING YOUR PEARLS
AND THRIVING

You have read this book all the way through and maybe you have even read it more than once. Now is the time to start using the pearls of wisdom so that you can begin achieving your own goals and capturing your own dreams. The pearls of wisdom do work. I know this because I've used them for twenty-five years and they have always worked for me.

The basic tenet for the ten pearls is the fact that you do get flashes, gut feelings, notions, hunches, impulses, and instincts all the time; and that these should be your guides as you go about your daily activities. This alone is fine. If you take it no further, this practice would be time well spent.

However, the major purpose of this book is to encourage you to use those same flashes, gut feelings, notions, hunches, impulses, and instincts to help you design road maps to your goals and dreams of success — whatever those happen to be for you. In this way you can modify and enhance your life so that you are fulfilled and not just drifting along making do with whatever happens to land in your lap. This book is about making your life better, easier, and more satisfying than it may be right now.

Another major purpose of this book is to show you that using the pearls of wisdom is easy. You don't have to do anything grueling or out of the ordinary. The pearls are simple and understandable. You can put them into practice without calling any undue attention to yourself.

Let's briefly review each of the pearls

1. BELIEVE. Do this in your heart. You can train yourself to react to anything that comes into your life with faith rather than with doubt. You can get up in the morning looking for-

ward to the day, eager with anticipation, and with confidence that you are going to be able to handle what comes to you. You can move from there to the point where you realize that you can actually control a lot of what comes to you; you can mold and shape your circumstances to your own specifications. From that base you then move to a state of expectation. You begin to know in your heart that as long as what you want will not abuse anyone else, it will come to you. And you will be alert to any opportunity that can assist you with gaining what you want.

2. REMEMBER. Recalling your past accomplishments, you begin to see yourself as someone who has been successful and to whom success is not unusual.

3. DECIDE. Now that you see yourself as capable of success based on your reflections about your past accomplishments, you go on to make up your mind about other things you want to achieve.

4. PLAN. Using those decisions, you find out what it takes to

get whatever it is you want and you begin to implement steps in that direction. Any time you come to a hitch or a roadblock, you refer back to your plan for insight and for encouragement.

5. ACTUATE. In your eagerness to achieve your goals you begin to act on every instinct that you feel about your goals. You can't stay still and just sit and dream. Your confidence has generated an excitement that pushes you to move toward your goals.

6. HABITUATE. Now you take small but significant actions toward your goal each day. Your aim is to do at least one action per day. And you reach the point that, if you have not taken at least one step toward your goal on any given day, you don't feel right.

7. PRETEND. This is where you have fun playacting. You visualize yourself, at least once a day, as you will be when you actually get to where you want to be.

8. REFINE. Using the mental picture of yourself as you will

be when you get to your goal, you begin to study that image so that you can discern any bumps or hitches that need to be attended to and resolved. And you set about doing any smoothing or preparing that you need to do so that when you achieve your goal you are ready for it in every way.

9. CLAIM. You convince yourself that what you want as long as it is not abusing anyone else is your due. Any doubt you have about deserving what you dream of is dissolved. This allows you to stay on the path to your dreams no matter what opinions you hear from others.

10. EXPAND. You continue to grow your desires and to reach further and further with your goal setting, using your pearls each step of the way. When you are grounded in the use of the ten pearls in your own life, you are ready to help others as you meet them on the pathway to their dreams.

Simple, natural, and easy to use

Pearls are formed by an oyster and are composed of layer

upon layer of a crystalline substance called nacre deposited around a grain of sand in the oyster's body. This happens in a steady, even tempo that is in tune with the nature of the elements involved.

That's how I see the pearls of wisdom. They are natural, made up of elements that we experience as part of life. There is nothing esoteric in this philosophy. The elements of the pearls of wisdom are as familiar to us as the act of breathing—we all have flashes, gut feelings, notions, hunches, impulses, instincts. *You* have them! In using the pearls of wisdom, what you are doing is paying attention to these elements in our daily lives and using them in a conscious way.

Your daily life is what you want to change; it's what you want to make better, easier, more satisfying and fulfilling. Start today to use the ten pearls of wisdom to achieve those goals and capture those dreams that you have been harboring for years. They can be yours– they are just waiting for *you*!

About the Author

ELEANOR JACOBS is a native of St.Louis, Missouri, and has a master's degree in social work (MSW) from St. Louis University. She is a Licensed Clinical Social Worker (LCSW) in California. During the past twenty years she has worked as the executive director for Catholic Social Service and the YWCA. From 1993–95 she served as the San Francisco Mayor's Office Homeless Coordinator, and she is currently the president and CEO of the United Way of Santa Clara County in the Silicon Valley area of northern California. She was named by the San Jose and Silicon Valley *Business Journal* as one of 1997's "Fifty Most Influential Businesswomen in the San Francisco Bay Area." Jacobs, her husband, and her son live in San Francisco and Santa Clara, California.